THE
EVERYTHING

EMOTIONAL INTELLIGENCE IN CHILDREN

Dear Reader,

I wandered into the area of emotional intelligence when researching materials to use in a psychology senior capstone course designed to help college students make a successful transition to the working world. In the fifteen years I've studied and taught about emotional intelligence since then, the research has grown and the positive benefits of high skill levels in emotional intelligence are much better known. I'm glad you've chosen to learn more about emotional intelligence and how to foster it in your children.

You'll notice that I often explain concepts like temperament or ground the information about emotional intelligence within the context of children's overall development. Knowledge of typical development and the uniqueness of your child will help you apply the concepts you learn much more effectively.

Some of the stories in this book are fictional but many of them are true with children's and parents' names changed to protect their identity. There's one notable exception to this pattern. The story about optimism in Chapter 17 includes a true story about a child named Justin. Unfortunately, his story is true. But, there's nothing at all unfortunate about his life or his optimism. I hope you will be inspired by his story.

Korrel

WELCOME TO THE

EVERYTHING

PARENT'S GUIDES

Everything® Parent's Guides are a part of the bestselling Everything® series and cover common parenting issues like childhood illnesses and tantrums, as well as medical conditions like asthma and juvenile diabetes. These family-friendly books are designed to be a one-stop guide for parents. If you want authoritative information on specific topics not fully covered in other books, Everything® Parent's Guides are your perfect solution.

Alerts

Urgent warnings

Facts

Important snippets of information

Essentials

Quick handy tips

Questions

Answers to common questions

When you're done reading, you can finally say you know **EVERYTHING**®!

PUBLISHER Karen Cooper

MANAGING EDITOR, EVERYTHING® SERIES Lisa Laing

COPY CHIEF Casey Ebert

ASSOCIATE PRODUCTION EDITOR Mary Beth Dolan

ACQUISITIONS EDITOR Brett Palana-Shanahan

SENIOR DEVELOPMENT EDITOR Brett Palana-Shanahan

EVERYTHING® SERIES COVER DESIGNER Erin Alexander

Visit the entire Everything® series at *www.everything.com*

THE
EVERYTHING®

PARENT'S GUIDE TO

EMOTIONAL INTELLIGENCE IN CHILDREN

How to raise children who are caring, resilient, and emotionally strong

Korrel Kanoy, PhD

Avon, Massachusetts

Published by
Adams Media, a division of F+W Media, Inc.
57 Littlefield Street, Avon, MA 02322. U.S.A.
www.adamsmedia.com

ISBN 10: 1-4405-5193-6
ISBN 13: 978-1-4405-5193-2
eISBN 10: 1-4405-5194-4
eISBN 13: 978-1-4405-5194-9

Printed in the United States of America.

10 9 8 7 6 5 4 3 2 1

This book is intended as general information only, and should not be used to diagnose or treat any health condition. In light of the complex, individual, and specific nature of health problems, this book is not intended to replace professional medical advice. The ideas, procedures, and suggestions in this book are intended to supplement, not replace, the advice of a trained medical professional. Consult your physician before adopting any of the suggestions in this book, as well as about any condition that may require diagnosis or medical attention. The author and publisher disclaim any liability arising directly or indirectly from the use of this book.

Many of the designations used by manufacturers and sellers to distinguish their product are claimed as trademarks. Where those designations appear in this book and F+W Media was aware of a trademark claim, the designations have been printed with initial capital letters.

This book is available at quantity discounts for bulk purchases.
For information, please call 1-800-289-0963.

Some of the examples and dialogues used in this book are fictional, and have been created by the author to illustrate disciplinary situations.

Dedication

Justin, this book is for you. Your gifts, both in intelligence and emotional intelligence, have inspired many people and taught them how to live life with joy, perseverance, and grace.

Acknowledgments

Many people—mostly my children or other children, adolescents, and college students—deserve credit for the content of this book. You provided the challenge and joy of parenting and teaching, and I learned much about my own emotional intelligence in the process. Also, I'd like to thank my spouse, Bobby, for his endless patience as "the need to write" took priority over other activities, especially when most of the alternatives would have been much more fun for him!

Emotional intelligence
(ĭ-mō′shə-nəl ĭn-tĕl′ə-jəns)
(n) A set of skills that helps children identify, appropriately express, and manage their emotions; develop effective relationships; cope with stress; adapt to change; and make good decisions.

Contents

Introduction

So what is emotional intelligence anyway? And, more important, how does it relate to your child's well-being? Does it help to shape your child's long-term success? Simply put, yes it matters—a lot—to emotional well-being and success! And, the good news is that you can teach children emotional intelligence skills. Children are not born with (or without) emotional intelligence skills. Rather, they develop these skills—or don't develop them—by modeling parents and other important adults (e.g. teachers, older siblings, grandparents). And, they learn EI skills—or not—by copying what they see on television, experiencing different events, learning from their mistakes, and by responding to different parenting styles. Their development of emotional intelligence largely rests in your hands.

Even though personality and emotional intelligence are very different, a child's basic temperament or personality will sometimes influence which EI skills are easier or harder to acquire. Think of it like learning to ride a bike—even though some children are more coordinated or have better balance and therefore learn more easily, almost every child can improve with practice and eventually learn to ride a bike. So, certain children, based on their temperament, will need more practice to be comfortable using a skill (e.g., a shy child may find assertiveness more challenging). You need to be realistic about the pace of improvement and remain patient and encouraging as you actively teach emotional intelligence skills.

You're probably getting the picture that you're teaching your child about emotional intelligence whether you mean to be or not. That's correct. Thus, paying attention to what you're teaching related to emotional intelligence should be a major priority for you as a parent. Reading this book and implementing the suggested strategies will help you to engage in *intentional* teaching of emotional intelligence rather than leaving the lessons to chance, or worse, interacting with children in ways that could inhibit their development of emotional intelligence. For example, if you say to your son "big boys don't cry," you are teaching him to suppress feelings of sadness. Yet, you may also give him free reign to vent his anger. Can boys only be mad and never sad? And, how does that combination affect their relationships with others? As some of you have witnessed or experienced, suppressing sadness and freely expressing anger will not help your son be effective in relationships as he matures into adulthood.

Or, if you're hovering too much over your children, doing things for them they can do for themselves, you're discouraging a different emotional intelligence skill, their independence. Children need to develop independence in order to separate from parents, whether it's to go to camp, to college, or to pursue a terrific job in another state as a young adult. Even if children do manage physical separation, they may be so emotionally dependent that they cannot handle the expectations of college or adult life—making decisions, managing money, or handling minor disappointments— without calling you for help or support.

The phrase *emotional intelligence* is relatively new, popularized in the mid-1990s by Daniel Goleman's book by that title. The concepts defining emotional intelligence and the associated skills, however, have been around for many years, allowing a strong research base to develop that details the advantages of well-developed emotional intelligence.

A child's emotional intelligence will likely be one of the strongest predictors of her ultimate success. A child with high emotional intelligence will be able to better understand and emotionally regulate herself, engage in more effective and empathic relationships with others, make better decisions, and be resilient and adaptive, allowing her to manage stress and life circumstances more effectively. There's plenty of research to support the notion that higher emotional intelligence is associated with better outcomes for children and teens, including improved academic performance and less problematic behaviors in school, enhanced self-confidence, and better emotional self-awareness.

The Everything® Parent's Guide to Emotional Intelligence in Children will teach you about emotional intelligence and how to develop it in your child. And, the appendices will give you tools, including a rating scale and an emotions chart, to better understand your child's current level of emotional intelligence.

CHAPTER 1

What Is Emotional Intelligence and Why Is It Important?

Simply put, emotional intelligence involves an array of skills that allow you or your child to understand and leverage emotions in ways that lead to more accurate self-awareness, greater confidence, more effective coping, stronger relationships, better decision-making, and more academic and work success. Emotional intelligence does not mean that your child is emotional or must tell others everything he's feeling. Rather emotional intelligence skills will allow your child to stand up to bullies, handle pressure, or become motivated to perform at his best—among many other things!

Is Emotional Intelligence Just a Trend?

Emotional intelligence has been around for a very long time. Early philosophers noted the importance of aspects of emotional intelligence, even though they did not use that term. Consider Plato's instruction to "Never discourage anyone . . . who continually makes progress, no matter how slow" (which would build self-regard) and his admonition to "Be kind, for everyone you meet is fighting a hard battle" which displays empathy. Aristotle's reflection that "Anybody can become angry—that is easy, but to be angry with the right person and to the right degree and at the right time and for the right purpose, and in the right way—that is not within everybody's power and is not easy" underscores the need for effective understanding and expression of emotion.

🅔❗ Alert

Emotional intelligence is not the same thing as common sense, nor is it something we improve upon just because of life experience. Skills like emotional intelligence must be learned and practiced.

By the 1920s, American psychologists were discussing social intelligence and which nonintellectual factors could predict success. In 1983, Harvard psychologist Howard Gardner presented the idea of "multiple intelligences" which included verbal and mathematical skills but also interpersonal and intrapersonal effectiveness. The term "emotional quotient" (EQ) was introduced by Reuven Bar-On in the 1980s as he developed an assessment tool to measure EQ. And, by the end of the 1990s the term "emotional intelligence" had been formally defined by many professionals. So, is emotional intelligence a trend that will soon disappear? Hardly. Do you know any trends that began with the earliest philosophers, still exist today and are still gaining momentum?

A Model of Emotional Intelligence

The emotional intelligence model shown here contains five major areas of emotional intelligence and sixteen separate skill areas. If you want your child to develop confidence, set and achieve goals, stand up to others when necessary, form strong and meaningful relationships, make good decisions, handle stress effectively, and be happy, then this book is for you!

The definitions for each of the sixteen emotional intelligence skill areas shown in the model are adapted from Steve Stein and Howard Book's popular book *The EQ Edge*, published in 2011.

Model of Emotional Intelligence

Reprinted with permission of Multi-Health Systems, August 2012.

 Alert

Self-esteem, self-confidence, self-concept, and self-regard all have slightly different meanings. Be sure you understand and apply the definition of self-regard as it's used in this book.

1. **Emotional self-awareness** involves the ability to recognize emotions as they are happening and know what causes those emotions. The child's ability to read others' reactions to her emotions is part of emotional self-awareness. Emotional self-awareness allows a child to answer the question "what's wrong?" when upset, and to tell you the cause for the distress; ironically, many children are effective at this skill and it's only when they hear things like "but you shouldn't feel that way because . . . " or "don't be so sensitive" that they stop telling you their feelings and about what's bothering them.
2. **Self-regard** involves understanding strengths and limitations, and accepting and respecting yourself despite your limitations. The third element of self-regard is your child's confidence level, which emerges primarily from self-acceptance and respect. Children high in self-regard do *not* brag, nor are they egotistical; rather, they possess an accurate understanding of strengths and limitations (e.g., I'm really good at math, but not as good in spelling), accept themselves as they are—neither being overly self-critical nor defensive when others point out their limitations; and, they strive to improve and are confident (not cocky) because of their clear understanding of their strengths and limitations.
3. **Self-actualization** encompasses striving to realize potential, setting appropriate goals and achieving them, and receiving satisfaction and meaning from pursuits. Behaviors evident in children might include trying out for a team, deciding to pursue a talent, and striving for improvement at school or in an activity they pursue. Children must experience joy and meaning from their pursuits to possess self-actualization; otherwise, if they are doing something to keep parents happy or because they believe it is expected of them, the joy will fade and in some cases, resentment builds.
4. **Emotional self-expression** includes the ability to express appropriate emotions verbally and nonverbally and for that

expression to be congruent. Children who can engage in healthy emotional expression will use words such as mad, sad, happy, or scared; and, their nonverbal actions will match their words.

5. **Independence** is the ability to be self-directed and function without too much dependence on others or an undue need for support or reassurance. Behaviors you might see in children include everything from a two-year-old saying "I'll do it myself" to a seven-year-old being comfortable spending the night at a friend's house, to a preteen who doesn't ask for help on homework until she really gets stuck.

6. **Assertiveness** involves the ability to express opinions, beliefs, and thoughts and to stand up for yourself in an appropriate and constructive way. Children as young as fifteen or sixteen months demonstrate assertiveness when they say "no" or refuse to eat a certain food they don't like the taste of. It's important for children to practice sharing opinions or standing up for themselves (e.g., expressing a preference for a light coat over a heavier one) if you expect them to do it when it really counts such as when confronted by a bully or pressured by friends to do something they know is wrong.

7. **Interpersonal relationship** involves developing relationships with others that involve mutuality, trust, and sharing. It includes the skill to build friendships and to be comfortable with others such as grandparents or teachers. Behaviors children might exhibit include everything from playing comfortably with other children, reaching out to friends, or being able to tell you something important such as something bad that happened to them at school or wanting to quit an activity that you value highly.

8. **Empathy** involves developing the awareness that others may have a different perspective and then trying to understand their perspective and the reasons for it. Appreciating the feelings others may be experiencing is a key part of empathy. Behaviors children might display include willingness to share a toy

without coaxing because they understand a friend wants to play with it, asking someone who is crying "what's wrong?" or, at an older age, being able to ask appropriate questions to help them understand someone else's feelings or behaviors. Empathy does not mean feeling sorry for someone or that you have to agree with their perspective.

9. **Social responsibility** involves the ability to be a cooperative, contributing, and constructive member of one's group(s). Cooperative behaviors you might see in children include doing their chores without constant reminders, willingness to share with peers or siblings who want to borrow something, helpfulness when asked and even when not asked, and, as they get older, a willingness to volunteer their time to help someone else.

10. **Problem solving** involves the ability to identify and define problems and then generate ideas for effective solutions. Behaviors you might see in children include telling you when they are struggling with something at school, on a sports team, or with a friend and then being willing to generate a list of potential solutions (with help from you). Also, commitment to solve the problem by implementing at least one of the solutions is important.

11. **Reality testing** involves the ability to distinguish between fantasy or hopes and what is real. Reality testing involves an accurate reading of the environment and facts without over- or under-reacting. Behaviors children might engage in include following family rules even when they don't want to (e.g., doing their homework before watching TV) because they understand the consequences of not doing so, or not denying things that are factual (e.g., believing a D grade was a good grade because lots of kids made a D), and not procrastinating on major projects or chores to the point that the task cannot get done well in the time allotted.

12. **Impulse control** involves resisting temptation, being patient, being willing to delay gratification, or not acting on impulses. Behaviors you may see in children include the ability to not overeat, not throw a tantrum, complete a less desirable event

before doing something that's fun (e.g., complete homework before getting on the computer), and show patience when completing a difficult task.

13. **Stress tolerance** includes the ability to withstand things that activate stress without falling apart, becoming internally agitated, or feeling overwhelmed. Behaviors you might see in children include not having "meltdowns" except on rare occasions, not being too fearful of new situations, events, or challenges, and being able to stay focused on the task at hand even in stimulating or stressful environments.

⊛ Essential

Don't try to protect children from stress. Instead, teach them appropriate coping strategies! This will help your children much more in the long run because they will have practiced handling stress and gain confidence as a result.

14. **Flexibility** involves being comfortable with change and adjusting emotions, thoughts, and behavior to changing situations. Behaviors you might see in children include beginning new things with excitement or a neutral response rather than too much anxiety, adjusting well to changes in the family (e.g., moving to a new house, having grandma come live with you, birth of a sibling), and being willing to try new things.

15. **Optimism** is the ability to remain positive and to persist when faced with adversity. Behaviors you might see in children include an attitude of "I can do better at this if I try hard enough" or a willingness to keep trying to master something that is difficult. Positive statements or positive ways of framing situations rather than negative ones (e.g., "practicing has helped me get better" rather than "I'm still not very good even though I practiced a lot") is also evidence of optimism.

16. **Happiness** includes the ability to feel satisfied with and enjoy life, being cheerful instead of somber. Behaviors include smiling, laughing, and wanting to engage as opposed to withdraw.

Why Emotional Intelligence (EI) May Be More Important Than IQ

You've been conditioned your whole life to pay attention to your grades, test scores, percentiles on standardized exams, and a whole array of other similar things. Thus, it's natural to believe that IQ (or intelligence quotient) is the key to success at every stage of life. It's not. But, don't misunderstand either. A higher IQ will make most types of learning easier for a child, will likely lead to better performance in school, may gain a child access to a gifted or talented program, and usually ensures higher scores on college entrance exams, which opens up more choices for your child.

Yes, you want your child's IQ to be as high as possible, but a high IQ alone doesn't guarantee success either in school or in life. That's where emotional intelligence comes in. A child with an average IQ who is highly motivated to do well (self-actualization), persists when work gets challenging (optimism), understands when she needs help (reality testing), asks for that help (assertiveness), and is disciplined enough to complete academic work carefully and on time (impulse control), will almost always outperform a child with above average or high IQ who is unmotivated, undisciplined, and unrealistic about the work required. If you were a teacher, which child would you prefer to teach?

How Do IQ and EI Contribute to Adult Success?

Studies of adults who were intellectually gifted as children reveal a mixed bag of success in the professional world. Some were highly successful in life and their careers, but others were not. The deciding factors often rested with their emotional intelligence skills. So, a higher IQ alone does not guarantee success and a lower IQ—but still within normal intelligence ranges—does not doom one to failure. It's EI that makes a bigger difference.

 Fact

There's very little relationship between IQ and emotional intelligence. So a high IQ child can have well-developed emotional intelligence, or he could be severely hampered by lower skills in emotional intelligence. Likewise, a child with a lower IQ may have very well-developed emotional intelligence skills, or poor skills in EI, which would amount to double jeopardy. IQ and emotional intelligence are two different and unrelated forms of intelligence.

Consider what multimillionaires said when Thomas Stanley asked them to rate factors that contributed to their success. In his book *The Millionaire Mind*, Stanley noted that multimillionaires rated the top five factors contributing to their success as: being honest, being highly disciplined, getting along with people, having a supportive spouse, and working harder than most people. Each of these factors reflects aspects of emotional intelligence. And what did the millionaires say about cognitive intelligence? It was ranked twenty-first out of thirty possible factors! While money earned is not the only or maybe even the most important measure of adult success, it's one way to measure success. And, notice that three of the top five factors dealt with relationships (honesty, getting along, supportive spouse) so it's likely that many of these millionaires also enjoyed successful relationships as well.

EI Continues to Develop; IQ Stops Developing

IQ can be influenced by many factors in a child's life including things such as prenatal nutrition, genetics, and how stimulating the early environment is for the child. But, by the end of the teenage years, brain development is almost finished and IQ is set.

EI, however, grows throughout most of adulthood, peaking in our fifties or sixties and only declining minimally until the eighties. Learning EI skills during childhood is like many other skills such as how to tie a shoe or ride a bike. Once learned, the skill never fades away completely, although it can get a little rusty if unused! And, because so many life circumstances give children opportunities to use their EI skills, this practice further solidifies the skill so that it's accessible even during the most challenging times.

🌟 Essential

Begin observing others when you're in the grocery store, at a child's soccer game, or in other public places. Chances are you will observe someone that you know to be very smart (IQ smart), but who makes of fool of himself by complaining vehemently to the cashier about how slowly the checkout line moved or screaming at a teenager who's refereeing the soccer game about a "missed" call. Put a mirror to your behavior in public. What do others see?

Emotional Intelligence and Research

Learning about just a few of the studies that have examined aspects of emotional intelligence in children should help maximize your motivation to teach these skills to your child. You may wonder why studies that look at teenagers or college students are relevant. There's a simple answer. The emotional intelligence your child develops now has important implications for future success.

One More Marshmallow, Please

Suppose you have a five-year-old child. Pretend that you've put a marshmallow on a plate in front of your child and said, "I've got to go wake up your sister and change her diaper. If you can stay here and not eat the marshmallow until I come back, I'll give you a second marshmallow." What do you think your child would do? Eat the marshmallow? Get up out of the chair to avoid the temptation? Beg you to eat it now? Cry? Or, think of ways to avoid the temptation and wait until you returned? If your child could do the latter, that shows excellent impulse control. Stanford psychologist Walter Mischel did such a study with preschool-aged children. While some gave in to the temptation to eat the marshmallow, others were able to delay gratification and get that coveted second marshmallow. What's interesting is what happened to these children as they grew older. The children who were able to wait experienced a variety of more positive outcomes as adolescents including better school performance (and not because they were smarter), better peer relationships, and higher ratings by teachers.

All of this occurred just because the child could wait to eat a marshmallow at age five? Children with better impulse control are more likely to stay on task during class time rather than goofing off with friends, complete their homework before playing, and work on a complex problem or project without losing patience. And, because impulse control involves the skill of avoiding rash behaviors, peer relationships are probably calmer and less likely to involve harsh words, hurtful teasing or other behaviors that, if the child thought before acting, may not happen at all. Any guesses what happened to the marshmallow eaters in adulthood? They were less likely to have achieved as much success at work as those who could wait and they experienced more trouble in their relationships.

Social Success and Popularity

Do you think emotional intelligence might be able to distinguish popular from unpopular preteens and teens? Zavala and colleagues compared highly popular children to those who were less popular but not the least popular. Although the popular group was *not* more effective in their social skills, they were significantly higher in their emotional intelligence skills. It makes sense that emotional intelligence skills such as understanding your emotions and how they may impact others, empathizing with friends, cooperating with others, avoiding rash behaviors, and being positive and cheerful might make a teen more popular. Who would want to be around someone for very long if they didn't have those skills?

 Fact

Research makes it clear that the maxim "money can't buy happiness" is very true. So, don't think giving your child lots of gifts or showering them with lots of material possessions will create lasting happiness.

School Success—Grades and Discipline

Yes, emotional intelligence seems to matter a lot, even in a situation that is almost exclusively focused on academic intelligence. A recent study, published in 2010, give a window through which to view emotional intelligence and academic success.

Researcher Karen Kohaut collected emotional intelligence scores, final grades for the academic year, and the number of discipline referrals middle-school children received. She found significant relationships between these preteens' emotional intelligence scores and both academic performance and number of school discipline problems. As you may have expected, children with higher emotional intelligence received fewer discipline referrals and earned better grades. There was no difference though in the emotional intelligence scores across racial or ethnic groups.

EI Goes to College

By now, it probably won't surprise you that emotional intelligence skills are predictive of college success. Emotional intelligence expert Steve Stein and his colleagues summarized research related to college students' success in their book *The Student EQ Edge:*

Emotional Intelligence and Your Academic and Personal Success. Even among the brightest students, such as those attending prestigious universities in the Ivy League, the EI skill of *optimism* can be a better predictor of college success than SAT scores. And, once in college, your child will have a much better chance of graduating if she is equipped with high impulse control, high social responsibility, moderate levels of independence and interpersonal relationship skills, high self-actualization, and high reality testing. In other words, if your child can delay gratification by studying before partying, gets involved in meaningful activities at her school (involvement on campus predicts graduation) and collaborates well with others on team projects, shows enough independence to separate from you without too much homesickness but not so independent she refuses to ask for help when needed, forms good and meaningful peer relationships but doesn't spend all her time hanging out with friends, sets academic goals, and is realistic about how well she's doing and what she needs to do to be more successful, then she has an excellent chance of both graduating and making better grades. So, one of the best investments you can make in your child's future is to teach her EI skills!

A Note about Bullying and Emotional Intelligence

As stories of bullying increase and some of the consequences become more severe (e.g., suicides, children under eighteen being charged with homicide), more adults are paying attention to what bullying is, what causes it, and why it continues.

Bullying is easy to distinguish from teasing. Teasing is directed at people we feel some affection for and the intent is playful and positive. An April Fool's Day prank will probably create laughter and positive feelings if the people involved care about each other. But other pranks, like posting false and harmful messages about someone on Facebook, are acts of bullying because the prank was intended to hurt someone or send a message motivated by dislike, intolerance, or disdain.

Application of emotional intelligence principles helps to understand all of the players in a bullying situation including bullies, victims, and observers. Bullies, in EI language, probably have lower self-regard (less self-acceptance and thus the need to diminish others), lower emotional self-awareness (lacks understanding of the motivation for bullying), lower empathy (cannot take the perspective of the victim), lower social responsibility (less cooperative, more likely to look out for himself first before thinking of others) and lower impulse control (cannot resist urges).

Victims, in EI language, may lack self-regard (which projects to others as low self-confidence) and emotional self-expression and assertiveness skills that would allow her to stand up to the bully. Victims may try to be too independent by not telling adults who could help intervene, and they may lack the problem-solving skills that could make bullying stop.

And, what about the EI skills of bystanders who watch the bullying, perhaps even laughing? They lack enough assertiveness to confront the bully and also lack a level of empathy that would allow them to help the victim. Their lack of independence prevents them from stepping out alone to try to address the problem—instead, they bend to peer pressure and become silent onlookers. They probably also lack some social responsibility—not thinking about the impact of the bullying within the "team" or group—and focus only on protecting themselves from bullying (which does show reality testing).

🛑 Alert

Bullying begins in elementary schools, so be cognizant of signs your child may give you that he's been bullied such as wanting to change schools, anxiety about going to school, not wanting to ride the bus home, or vague reasons not to play with neighborhood children.

A well-constructed emotional intelligence curriculum could help reduce bullying by giving onlookers and victims the skills to stand up to the bully. And the bully would learn empathy and other skills that would allow him to feel more connection with the victim rather than continuing to label that person as an outcast who deserves to be bullied.

What about Your Emotional Intelligence?

As you can imagine, the better your EI skills, the more your child will learn by watching how you handle situations. If you fall apart when stress gets high, treat kids more harshly when you're mad, have buttons your kids can push that you didn't even know existed, or flounder with a lack of self-confidence, then how can you expect your children to react differently?

 Question

How can I be sure about my level of emotional intelligence?
The only way to be sure about your level of emotional intelligence is to complete an assessment, preferably a 360 one, that is both reliable and valid. If you are interested in completing an assessment that uses the same model of emotional intelligence used in this book, contact Multi-Health Systems for a list of certified administrators (*http://ei.mhs.com*), or contact the author at *www.developmentalassociates.com*.

Research with adults about emotional intelligence indicates that EI benefits you in every arena of your life. Stein and Book in their engaging book published in 2011, *The EQ Edge*, document many positive outcomes for adults with well-developed EI skills including:

- At work, whether a teacher or lawyer, a banker or debt collector, an athlete or artist, or a CEO or accountant, EI skills are predictive of success in a variety of careers with the five best predictors of overall work success being self-actualization, happiness, optimism, self-regard, and assertiveness.

- In marriage, those with higher EI report greater levels of marital happiness; and the best predictor of this greater marital satisfaction includes EI skills such as an individual's happiness, self-regard, self-awareness, self-actualization, and reality testing. In other words, the happiest marriages included individuals who were happy, understood their strengths and *weaknesses* (thus, probably being more willing to say "I'm sorry" or take responsibility for their part of a problem), understood their own emotions and what triggered them (making it easier to identify needs and wants or to be clear during arguments), set and achieved personal goals that gave life meaning and satisfaction, and were realistic about marriage, neither fantasizing about it nor blaming the marriage for all of one's individual woes (reality testing).

- In finding and keeping a job, those who are chronically unemployed during most of their adult years score lower than employed individuals in assertiveness, optimism, emotional self-awareness, reality testing, and happiness. You may be thinking, "Well, of course they would score lower on these skills—they're unemployed!" But, the fact that these individuals were *never* employed consistently implies that these lower EI skill areas may have been present for years and thus a possible reason for the unemployment.

- In coping with a chronic illness, adults who participated in an EI skill-development class reported an increased quality of life and well-being compared to those with the same illness that did not go through the EI class.

- In maintaining health, those who exercise more also have higher EI skills. As you can imagine, the ability to set and achieve goals (i.e., self-actualization) probably plays a role in whether someone sticks to a New Year's pledge to exercise more or not.

CHAPTER 2

A Closer Look: Case Studies of EI in Children

The case studies cited in this chapter are fictional. Yet, they represent often-occurring patterns in families. Each case study will focus on a target child or children. As you read each case study, imagine how the child's experiences—including parenting styles, childhood environment, personality, and other factors—contribute to the child's developing EI skills. Form hypotheses about how EI skills will affect how the child deals with difficult challenges, where the child is likely to excel, and what could have been done differently to promote higher emotional intelligence. Come back to these case studies after you have completed reading the book to see if your thoughts have changed. They should!

Case Study: Building Independence

Joey was the fourth child in a family with three older sisters who were between four and eight years older than Joey. The whole family was thrilled when he was born; his parents wanted a male child and his three older sisters loved having a living "baby doll" to play with. From the beginning, Joey was a little fussy, but his sisters could always provide enough distraction and entertainment to change his mood. They doted on him, handing him his pacifier, reaching things he pointed to and generally providing constant entertainment. His speech development was somewhat delayed, but no one was worried about him because they knew he didn't have to say much in order to communicate his needs. He would simply cry, gesture, or point and usually someone in the family knew what he wanted.

As a toddler, Joey got really frustrated by things he couldn't do that his sisters did such as swim, go on a bike ride, or write his name. He was constantly trying to keep up with them but couldn't. Sometimes he would just dissolve in tears. Usually someone quickly dropped what he or she was doing to attend to Joey, distracting him with food or doing something exciting like taking him on a "piggy back" ride around the house. His speech improved, but he lagged behind other kids in his vocabulary and even how he pronounced his words. Joey's parents were so busy with work and having four children that when he went through the stage of throwing tantrums, they usually just gave in to what he wanted.

When it came time to go to kindergarten, Joey was excited because now he would ride a school bus like his sisters. But, the first week of school did not go so well. He got frustrated when his teacher and friends kept asking him to repeat things because they couldn't understand him and also when the teacher made him do things for himself, like open his juice box or hang up his coat.

Question

Are tantrums to be expected with preschool children?
Tantrums will be more frequent for children who have not been taught how to use words to express their needs or feelings. And, it's also likely that if a child gets upset enough, he may have a tantrum even if he is skilled at communicating with words. The key to ridding your child of tantrums is to provide healthier ways to express feelings and not give in to his demands.

By the second week of school, Joey was throwing a tantrum in the morning because he didn't want to go to school. When his parents asked him what was wrong, Joey didn't know how to explain it. Finally, they just told him to quit crying, that he was going to have to go to school; things would get better they reassured him. And, although things did get better, Joey still had a hard year.

EI Analysis for "Building Independence"

You probably noticed some things that Joey's family could have done differently to help him develop emotional intelligence skills that in turn would have made his kindergarten experience much easier. When infants are young, they only have two ways of communicating; first they can cry and later that first year they add gestures such as pointing or holding their arms out in a gesture that says "pick me up." It's absolutely fine to respond to those gestures, but it is also important to encourage verbal communication. For example, label objects and the child's feelings as you respond. If the child whines and points to a container of Cheerios just out of reach, label the behavior and the emotion. Saying something like "You want the Cheerios; are you frustrated that you can't reach them?" This will help the child develop his vocabulary so that he can communicate needs verbally starting sometime during the second year of life. And, adding a comment about the emotion the child is probably feeling will help him to do likewise for himself as he ages. Even if your guess about the emotion is incorrect— maybe Joey was mad and not frustrated—the mere act of teaching the child to pay attention to his emotions and how they influence behavior is what's important. In EI language, you would be teaching emotional self-awareness, probably one of the most important EI skills because it's foundational to development of some of the other EI skills.

Back to Joey. How could his family have helped him with developing more independence? Teaching him how to do things for himself would have had multiple benefits. First, it would have increased his skills—whether in learning to dress himself or open a straw—and more important, it would have increased his belief that he is capable of doing things on his own, which builds self-regard. Children will confront many new challenges in school and the more success he's had at mastering new skills, the more independent he will be when faced with new challenges.

 **Essential**

Think about how you can make it easier for your child to practice independence. Buy Velcro shoes instead of tie-up shoes and clothes with big buttons that are easy to work. Put a stool by the kitchen counter so that your three-year-old can deliver her plate to the counter. Make environmental changes that support independence!

Did you notice that Joey may have developed some intolerance to stress? When you protect your child from stressors, they don't get practice dealing successfully with stress. And, since everyone faces stress every day, protecting children from demands is exactly the antithesis of what you should do. If two children are arguing about a toy, give them a chance to work things out before intervening. Or, if a child is experiencing frustration learning to button clothing, stay patient yourself and offer encouragement. If you jump in and rescue your child by performing a task for him that he needs to learn to do, you're stifling independence and teaching him that someone will come to the rescue at the first sign of difficulty (stress).

Did you notice that Joey's impulse control needed development? It's not helpful to be unrealistic about children's ability to tolerate frustration and thus, don't expect a four-year-old to stand in line for thirty minutes or wait for an hour to eat when she's very hungry. Every toddler will throw tantrums; your role is to teach a child other ways to handle her impatience or frustration. You can't expect a child to suddenly develop good impulse control if the skill has not been practiced. When small frustrations arise—a five-minute wait to check out at the grocery store—take the opportunity to teach the child how to deal with it. Sing a song, point to different things in the cart and label them, or play a simple game. As the child gets older, put more responsibility on her to handle the frustration without losing control. Think about an adult you know who sends rash e-mails or texts when angry, can't control the urge to eat or spend, or can't wait a realistic amount of time for things she wants. Learning impulse control will prevent many problems in adulthood that arise from rash or impatient behaviors.

 Fact

Joey clearly lacked independence when he began school. The *authoritative style of parenting,* which you will read about throughout this book, encourages children to develop appropriate amounts of independence.

Case Study: Choosing Activities

Eight-year-old Sara had always loved the water. She happily splashed as an infant in the bathtub, loved jumping into a pool as a preschooler, and even joined her neighborhood swim team during the summer she was six. Her skills progressed rapidly and by the time she was eight, she was finishing first in most of her races. Sara's parents were approached by a coach for the year-round swim club about signing Sara up for the RACERS. Her parents recognized her talent and agreed that joining a year-round team would enable her to develop her talent. Besides, with only three required practices a week, the extra exercise would be good for her and help her sleep better. So, her parents signed her up.

Sara, who loved swimming, at first was excited about joining the year-round team. But as the weeks passed, the practices seemed boring. Plus, her parents had refused to let her play soccer again this fall as she had for the last three years. They thought it would be too much emphasis on sports with not enough time for homework or just being a normal eight-year-old.

So, while her friends all went to soccer games on Saturday mornings where they had lots of fun, Sara spent an hour and a half at swim practice, which wasn't nearly as much fun. That spring, Sara again asked to play soccer and again was told no. The most important meets for year-round swimmers occurred in March and soccer would interfere with one of her swim practices each week. Plus she would have missed lots of soccer games to go to swim meets.

Alert

Most parents who try to "coach" their kids believe they do so because they want the best for their child. But, there are plenty of parents sitting in the stands or standing on the sideline who want the best for their child. What separates those parents? A "coaching" parent probably has very strong values, needs, or past experiences driving her behavior. So, it's important to examine your own emotions around your child's participation in sports or any other competitive realm. What's driving you to coach your child?

When it came time for the big swim meet in March, Sara was very excited. The meet was held in a different city so her parents and younger sister piled in the car and they all traveled three hours away, staying in a hotel that weekend. Sara was really nervous and got an upset stomach the first morning of the meet. And, she didn't swim well. Her parents were supportive but also had lots of advice for her. "Take some deep breaths when you're waiting your turn to swim," reminded her father. "And, don't forget to kick hard the whole race," added Mom. Day two of the meet went about the same. Sara was nervous, maybe even more than the first day. Though she did okay and raced her best times ever, she didn't finish first (or even second or third) in any of her events. Her parents, concerned that she wasn't progressing fast enough, asked to meet with the coach. The coach suggested that Sara add one practice a week. When her parents told her about the change, Sara began to cry. She had been hoping to join the soccer team now that the big swim meet was over and there wouldn't be another one for a while. But, she didn't mention to her parents that going to an extra day of practice didn't seem like nearly as much fun as playing soccer with her friends. Instead, she kept going to practice.

EI Analysis for "Choosing Activities"

Sara's parents were well intentioned but not helpful to Sara when it came time to develop key aspects of her emotional intelligence. Self-actualization involves developing goals and then receiving meaning and satisfaction from achieving those goals. A child must learn to choose her own goals; but, well-meaning parents often choose goals for a child for a variety of reasons including the child's talents or the parents' belief that one activity is better for their child than another. If the child prefers doing something else though, it's unlikely she'll try as hard or stay with the activity as long as she would have if the activity had been her choice. And she'll feel more pressure because she knows how important it is to you.

Also, our self-regard comes from a realistic sense of our strengths and weaknesses. Expectations that are too high or feedback that is too picky (some would say critical) can diminish self-regard. Was it realistic for Sara's parents to expect her to finish in the top three against better competition than she faced in the summer league? And, was it helpful to Sara for them to point out things she was doing wrong, even if the parents were correct? Your role as a parent is to encourage and support your child. Point out what she did right and know that the coach will give her more balanced feedback. And, if she asks for your opinion about what she could have done better, it's okay to give it to her. Or, you can always ask what the coach suggested to her to make sure she's not just getting all praise or all criticism. Providing only praise could give children a false sense that they don't have any need for improvement, making it harder for them to accept any feedback as they get older, whereas too much criticism erodes positive energy and confidence.

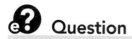 **Question**

How can I deliver criticism without upsetting my child?
First, think about it as feedback (neutral connotation) and not criticism (negative connotation). Second, couch your comments in descriptive language, not evaluative language. "I noticed you haven't taken your dirty uniform to the laundry as we agreed you would. I'm expecting you to do that."

What else did you notice? Do you let your child make choices about what she wants to do? Sara wanted to play soccer and at first was assertive about her desire. But, when her wishes weren't respected, she gave up, in essence learning that her opinion didn't matter. As she grows older, it will be very important to make sure your daughter can state her desires, set boundaries with others who are being pushy, or take up for herself when pressured by others.

Some of you may be thinking, "But I'm the parent. Certainly I know better than my child does what's best for her!" For many things that's true. Insisting that your child hold your hand while crossing the street or do her homework reflects good parenting. That's very different though, than telling your child what activities she must join or what she cannot join even though that's what she wants. There will always be athletic parents who give birth to a child who prefers the fine arts and artistic parents who give birth to a remarkably athletic child. Or, parents who love tennis and give birth to a child who wants to play soccer. Follow your child's lead about what activities she participates in and it will help build her self-actualization (it's easier to get excited about a goal she chooses for herself), self-regard (confidence that she knows herself well enough to choose well) and even her emotional self-awareness (knowing what makes her happy and what doesn't).

You may be wondering about reinforcing a child's assertiveness. Shouldn't parents be in charge? Of course you're in charge. People in charge have the responsibility to protect, teach, and nurture ones entrusted to their care. Thus, teaching assertiveness is perfectly compatible with your parental role. Which would you rather have—a child who is never allowed to be assertive and then resists your influence indirectly and perhaps defiantly (i.e., rebelling as a teen), a child who never develops any ability to express her needs or stand up to others (i.e., becoming passive and thus vulnerable to mistreatment by others), or a child who communicates clearly and appropriately what she wants?

 **Essential**

As you read about assertiveness throughout this book, remember that it never involves an intent to harm someone else, only to stand up for oneself in appropriate ways. Thus, it's hard to imagine that assertiveness could be disrespectful.

The above scenario also teaches lots of lessons about empathy, which involves the ability to take someone else's perspective. Did Sara's parents ever try to understand why she wanted to play soccer so badly? After all, she didn't ask to quit swimming, just to play soccer. If her parents don't ask questions about why soccer is so important to her, it indirectly communicates that it's not important to understand someone else's point of view. How will Sara develop empathy skills if this is what she observes at home? She probably won't; at least not as well as she would have if her parents had tried to understand her perspective. After all, she was an eight-year-old asking to play soccer with her friends a few months out of the year, not a sixteen-year-old who was dropping out of school! If her parents continue to ignore her perspective and pay attention only to their perspective, she's likely to mimic their behavior in her interactions with others. Needless to say, that won't help Sara's relationships in the future.

Finally, this case study serves as a reminder about the value of interpersonal relationships. Sara understands that even as an eight-year-old. She wants to spend time with friends doing something they mutually enjoy. Developing relationship skills may be one of the most important tasks of childhood. So, when children are asking to "practice" this skill by spending more time with friends, encourage their efforts!

 Essential

> Be sure not to overschedule your child. More and more activities are available to children as young as three or four. A good rule of thumb is to involve them in no more than two activities a week for most of the elementary years. And, there's no reason to start a child in such activities until she's five or six.

Case Study: Learning to Make Good Decisions

As you know, life is full of decisions—do you stay home to rear your children or return to work? Do you take a promotion that will relieve financial pressure and give you more meaningful work but simultaneously increase your time away from home? In order to navigate the more challenging decisions of adulthood, you must practice and then practice some more as children.

Consider the case of four-year-old Stephon. Each morning his mother carefully laid out what clothes he would wear to day care, robbing him of even a simple decision of choosing clothes. You may be thinking—well what if Stephon wanted to wear stripes with plaids? Or wear shorts on a day that's too cold for shorts? Or wear something that looks shabby to you, but he finds comfortable? Think about it this way—every decision you make as an adult has the potential for rewards or consequences. Practice making small decisions during childhood gives your child the skills to navigate the more difficult decisions that come later in life.

Stephon also didn't get any say so in what foods he ate or what TV shows he got to watch. The parents, although well intentioned in their belief that they knew what was best, removed all practice opportunities for making decisions. Putting restrictions on some TV shows (such as no violence or sexual content) is necessary and reflective of caring parents, but choosing what a child can watch out of all of the remaining programs assumes too much control over decisions.

EI Analysis for "Learning to Make Good Decisions"

Go back to Stephon. Suppose he does choose to wear shorts on a cold day. What's the worst that will happen? He'll get cold, but no, he won't get sick. (Ask your pediatrician—children get sick from viruses and bacteria, not from becoming too cold or getting rained on. The only exception would be if the child was *already ill* with a virus and then got too cold; that might make things worse.) So, let's suppose Stephon did get cold during the hour-long outdoor play time at his day care center. That will help him develop his reality testing skills. In other words, he'll learn to pay attention to information (e.g., Does it feel cold outside? What kind of clothes are my parents wearing?) that could help him make a better decision.

Some child psychologists have used the terms "natural consequences" and "logical consequences" to explain how children can learn from their choices (decisions). For example, if a child insists on wearing shorts and then gets very cold during outside play time, that would be a "natural consequence" (the consequence occurs naturally without the need for any adult intervention). Such consequences may make the child think twice before making the same decision again.

ⓔ✱ Essential

Logical and natural consequences can be used as discipline strategies and are typically very effective. You'll hear more about these strategies throughout the book.

A logical consequence requires some adult intervention, but the consequence is still related to the child's decision or behavior. For example, if a child makes a decision to sneak some cookies and eats too many, the child may get sick (a natural consequence) or the parent may choose to not buy cookies (a logical consequence). In both scenarios, the child's decision resulted in consequences that helped him get better at reality testing. The emotional intelligence skill of reality testing involves collecting information and then interpreting it accurately in support of good decision making. So, if you're a child who got very cold the last time you wore shorts, would you be more or less likely to wear shorts again on a cold day? We need to let children experience the consequences of their decisions rather than protecting them from such. Experience is a great teacher!

Case Study: Developing Flexibility and Optimism

It's sad to see children give up too easily, become overly anxious about events, or be afraid of change. Persistent behavior and an optimistic view can help children overcome many obstacles, which will lead to healthier self-regard.

Consider the case of Maria. As an only child, she and her parents developed very comfortable routines around their family life. Maria's dad always got an early start to the day, waking Maria up to kiss her goodbye and then immediately leaving for the gym before he began his work day. Maria's mom always cooked her a hot breakfast and then took her to school. After picking up Maria after school, they would go home, make a snack together and then sit down to do homework. Homework was followed by an hour of outside play or reading and then watching TV while her mom made dinner. They ate dinner together as a family at 6 P.M. And so on, with routines set up for bath, bedtime reading, and lights out by 8 P.M.

Because of some changes in their family circumstances, Maria's mom had to begin working full-time when Maria was eight. A trained nurse, Maria's mom chose to work a 7 A.M. to 7 P.M. schedule at the local hospital on Monday, Tuesday, and Wednesday. On those days, the family schedule changed dramatically. Maria was awakened by her dad and instead of a hot breakfast, she ate cereal. He dropped Maria off at a neighbor's house to wait for the school bus. And after school, Maria had to ride the bus home and was met by a high school student who stayed with her until her dad got home from work at about six. Dinner changed a lot on those days—Maria and her dad tried to wait until 7:30 P.M. to eat with her mom, but she got way too hungry and was very whiney by the time dinner started. And, waiting so late interfered with her nightly bath and bedtime routine.

Even though these changes were explained to Maria, her parents framed the changes with phrases such as "We wish mommy didn't have to go back to work" and "This is going to be really hard for all of us" and "Riding the bus probably won't be as fun as having mommy take you, but lots of kids do it." Her parents were expressing their honest thoughts and feelings, but they were doing so in a negative way that would undoubtedly make things more difficult for Maria. And, they could not be absolutely sure the bus ride wouldn't be fun, so there's no reason to frame it that way!

It's not surprising that Maria became extremely anxious and even uncooperative with her parents when the new schedule started. She cried every morning about having to ride the bus and in the afternoon sometimes refused to do her homework with the babysitter. She whined a lot during the evening because she was both physically and emotionally exhausted. And, all of a sudden, she was finding it harder to fall asleep. Her whining increased the conflict level with her parents and made getting her homework done without an argument a long-ago memory.

 **Question**

What is the best way to prepare children for change?
Children need you to explain change in a neutral or positive way, be honest with them, and keep the details simple. They'll ask more questions if they want more information. You'll learn more about how to build the EI skill of flexibility, or adaptation to change, in Chapter 15.

EI Analysis for "Developing Flexibility and Optimism"

So what happened? Change. And, change that was framed very negatively. Don't misunderstand: Children need structure and routines. And, they also need practice dealing with changing circumstances so they will learn to adapt to change rather than fear it. Sometimes change leads to something much better or more fun. Because of their inborn temperaments, some children are more cautious about new circumstances and thus more unsettled by them. Routines become very comfortable and despite their value, routines that are never varied make it harder to adjust when unexpected change does occur. Instead of protecting children from change, introduce it with positive framing (optimism) and with support (empathy). For example, Maria's parents could have talked to one of the neighbors to find out more about the bus ride and then given her factual information (as opposed to their opinions) such as "your friends Kayla and Shawna ride that bus and have room for you to sit with them" or "the bus driver gives every kid a funny nickname" or "a lot of the kids get most of their homework done on the bus, leaving more time for play."

And, if you are going to share information other than facts, try to frame the situation in positive terms, helping the child understand good things that may happen. The bus ride was framed in a negative way—not as much fun as being taken by mommy—when it could have been framed positively. Describe the opportunity to make new friends rather than focusing on not being with mom.

In addition to not being able to adjust to the changes (which is the EI characteristic of flexibility), Maria also experienced more stress—and that began to affect her sleep patterns and her temperament, leading to an increase in conflict with her parents. Flexibility, or the ability to adapt to changing circumstances, and optimism, the ability to frame things positively and persevere, are two key ingredients of stress management. So, if a child possesses neither of these EI skills, she will be more stressed, creating a whole host of additional challenges.

The case studies in this chapter highlight the fact that loving, involved parents who want only the best for their children are not necessarily fostering the most well-developed emotional intelligence skills. Thus, it's important for you to examine what EI skills you model for your child, your parenting style, and your discipline strategies and how each of these is contributing to your child's emotional intelligence.

CHAPTER 3

Emotional Self-Awareness

L ots of people think that "emotional intelligence" means being "emotional" all the time. That belief represents a significant misunderstanding of the concept. Instead, emotional intelligence applied to your child involves her understanding what causes her emotions, how her emotions impact herself and others around her, why emotions motivate certain behaviors, and what she can do to leverage her emotions to help her in any given situation. Before your daughter can do any of that, she must first be aware of when she is experiencing an emotion; thus, emotional self-awareness provides a foundation for developing other emotional intelligence skills.

What Is Emotional Self-Awareness?

Emotional self-awareness involves three components: understanding what emotion you are experiencing in the moment you experience it (not hours or days later), knowing what triggered that emotion, and finally, being aware of the impact of your emotions on others. Even though these skills may sound very lofty for children, it's never too early to begin teaching children EI skills. Emotional self-awareness does *not* mean that you are teaching your children to be too emotional; rather, it means teaching them to recognize their emotions as they occur and then make proactive choices about what to do, rather than reacting to emotions in a blind or impulsive way.

 Fact

Children become aware of their physical bodies at birth. For example, they respond with a stronger sucking movement to a finger rubbing their cheek than to their own fist hitting it. And, they are aware of a general feeling of "discomfort" at birth, which is what makes them cry when hungry, tired, or in need of a diaper change.

Why Learn Emotional Self-Awareness?

Teaching your child how to identify, manage, and leverage emotions will help him solve problems, stay motivated, and maintain healthy relationships. People are biologically wired to experience emotions that arise in one of the more primitive parts of the brain, the limbic system. Your child may see something that triggers a sad memory, hear something that makes him mad, or think about something that makes him worried, and so forth. The question becomes, *not* whether emotions occur in your child, but how will your child respond to those emotions? If your child identifies an emotion when it first occurs and then "forwards" it to the frontal lobe—which is responsible for reasoning, judgment, and decision-making—he has a much better chance of reacting effectively to that emotion.

Young children who don't learn to "forward" their emotions to the frontal lobe are held captive by more extreme, unchecked behaviors such as hitting, screaming, or throwing things. Your role as a parent is to teach the child how to become aware of an emotion as it is occurring and then help the child decide how to respond to the emotion effectively rather than reacting in rash ways.

Think back to the case study about Maria's situation. Her mother had to begin a full-time job out of necessity after years of being available to Maria full time. For many mothers, this would understandably cause some anxiety, sadness, or frustration. Those emotions, if you're unaware of them, will undoubtedly affect how you present this new situation to your child. The power behind these emotions becomes palpable, seeping through into your behavior, leading you to say or do things that are not helpful to your child or that you may later regret.

Essential

More than half of adults are unable to cue into emotions when they are first activated; rather, it takes a buildup in intensity or a prolonged activation of the emotion for many adults to become aware of it. Awareness in the moment makes it much easier to leverage your emotions to help yourself.

But, if you stopped to take stock of your feelings—say you are indeed anxious about this big change—then you can purposefully decide how to deal with your anxiety. Go back to Maria's parents. If they recognized their anxiety, they could do constructive things about it such as calling other parents to find out more about the bus ride, thus allowing them to frame things more positively with Maria. And, big changes such as Maria was about to experience will undoubtedly create strong emotions in her as a child, making this a teachable moment about how to better understand and leverage her emotions.

Conversation between Maria and her parents that recognizes each person's emotional reactions to the situation will accomplish two major objectives: first, it will make the upcoming transition *easier* (hiding emotions and not talking about them does not typically make them easier to handle), and second, it will develop Maria's emotional self-awareness. A bonus element is that the parents will be modeling emotional self-awareness and sending a message that such is a typical part of daily life.

Mastering the Parts of Emotional Self-Awareness

Remember that effective skill in emotional self-awareness involves three components: identifying and labeling feelings, understanding what triggered the emotion, and understanding how your emotional reaction will impact others. Each piece is critical to effective emotional self-management and to building positive relationships with others.

Alert

Be very careful not to project your emotions about any situation onto your child. For example, if your child has been bullied, you may be furious. You need to handle your emotional reaction separately from helping your child identify and understand the emotion he is experiencing.

Step One: Identifying and Labeling Feelings

Take the case of six-year-old Juan. When faced with mild bullying by kids in his class, he might become very mad, or perhaps embarrassed, scared, or sad. Different children react to the same event with different emotions. Thus, it's not the event by itself that triggers an emotion; rather, the emotion triggered depends on values the child has learned as well as life experiences. So, if Juan has been bullied a lot and has a hard time making new friends, he may feel sad. If there are other kids in the class Juan wants to play with and those kids witness the bullying, Juan may feel embarrassed.

Or, if Juan has been trained to always "fight back" and "take up for yourself," the bullying may make him mad. In Juan's case, let's suppose the bullying scares him. Only Juan knows which emotion (or emotions) is triggered. It's your job as a parent to discern which emotion has been activated in your child rather than telling your child how he should feel.

Step Two: Understanding What Caused the Emotion

You may think that the cause of the emotion is obvious—he was subjected to bullying. And yes, that's what *caused an emotional reaction, but it does not explain which emotion* Juan would experience. Not every child would have responded with the same emotion or even behaviors that Juan did. It's important for kids to begin paying attention to why a certain emotion was triggered—rather than another one—because that can empower them to change their emotional reaction or more importantly, to change their behavioral reaction. In Juan's case, let's suppose he's scared (but not mad, embarrassed, or sad) because he's very small for his age and the kids making fun of him are big and two of them also ride his bus.

 **Essential**

Most of what causes you to experience one emotion rather than another one in a given situation relates to your values and past experiences. For example, if you value respect and tolerance and have personally witnessed bullying as a teen, you may become very angry. On the other hand, if safety is a primary value and you've seen the scars others carry from bullying, your emotional reaction is more likely to be fear or anxiety. Effective emotional management involves knowing your values and understanding how your past experiences have shaped your emotional reactions in the present.

Step Three: Understanding How Your Emotions Affect Others

As soon as the bullying started, Juan looked away quickly, backed up, looked around for the teacher, and went over and sat very close to her. If a child is scared, a common response is to withdraw, retreat, or look for a safe area, such as beside a teacher or parent. But, that behavior typically reinforces the child who did the bullying. The bully knows that a retreat means the other child is scared. The bullying "worked" because it was designed to upset the target. Juan's retreat only verified his distress. The bullying is *not* Juan's fault, but his reaction to it may contribute to additional bullying.

 Fact

Even in infancy, children begin to understand the meanings of others' emotional signals. This is why they get more irritable if you're anxious. A key part of emotional self-awareness is recognizing the impact of your emotions on others. Your infant is watching you! Think about what she sees.

So what does Juan need to understand about his emotion of fear in this situation? He needs to understand that his behavioral responses to fear will likely increase the bullying, not decrease it. If he wants to stop the bullies, he may need to learn other behaviors that will communicate different messages to them. Notice, the advice is not to try to change the child's feeling (you cannot talk him out of being scared); rather, it's to change how he reacts to his fear.

You may be wondering how this scenario would be any better if Juan recognized his emotion as fear, knew why he was scared, and realized that acting afraid might reinforce the bullying. The first two responses (fear) and understanding the cause of the fear—those guys are bigger than I am, two of them ride my bus and I've seen them pick on other kids—give Juan the opportunity to think about how he will react. If he realizes that showing fear will make things worse, he may be able to choose a different behavior such as staying in his seat while ignoring the other boy, not making eye contact, and staying focused on his work. All of those responses will rob the other kid of the effect he wanted. While this is not guaranteed to stop bullying on the spot, it at least helps Juan be more in control of his behaviors. Choosing any of the reactions that don't show fear first requires Juan to be able to label his emotional reaction as fear, know why he felt scared rather than mad, sad, or some other emotion, and finally, understand that showing his fear by retreating may lead to more bullying, not less.

 Alert

Examine any biases you may have about boys learning to understand their emotions and then get rid of those biases! Juan would have reacted more effectively to the bullying if he was encouraged to understand how it made him feel and how he could have reacted differently to those feelings.

Practicing Emotional Self-Awareness Development

You're probably wondering if it's realistic to teach children to engage in the level of self-awareness described above. The answer is yes, but it takes lots of practice, with adults helping children to explore, label, and understand their feelings and then discussing possible ways to respond to various feelings. Kids will begin mastering emotional self-awareness if they are guided by adults such as Juan's father did in the conversation below.

Dad: Juan, how was school today?

Juan: Not so good.

Dad: What made it "not so good" for you?

Juan: The mean kids in my class.

Dad: What did those kids do to make you think they're mean?

Juan: Picked on me.

Dad: That must have felt yucky.

Juan: Yeah.

Dad: What did they do?

Juan: They called me a runt and made fun of my glasses.

Dad: That probably didn't feel so good. How did you feel when that happened?

Juan: I don't know. But, two of them ride my bus. I don't want to ride the bus anymore.

Dad: Hmm, sounds like you might be scared of these guys. Are you?

Juan: Yeah.

Dad: I'm glad you told me. Do you think they know you're scared?

Juan: I don't know.

Dad: Well, what did you do when they bullied you?

Juan: I went and sat by the teacher.

Dad: I bet that made you feel safer. What did those other boys do after you sat by the teacher?

Juan: They laughed and pointed at me until the teacher told them to stop.

Dad: What happened on the bus ride home? Anything?

Juan: Yeah, they called me a baby for going to sit by the teacher.

Dad: So going to sit by the teacher made them call you a baby. That must have hurt. I see why you said that school was "not good" today.

Juan: Yeah.

Dad: Let's talk about other things you could do if those kids bother you again.

Question

Should you use the words "bully" or "bullying" in your conversation with your child such as Juan's dad did with him? Wouldn't that make Juan more afraid?

"Let the truth be good enough" is a valuable maxim in parenting. Bullying can range in intensity from mild to horrific but what defines something as bullying is the intent to harm. Your child's emotional reaction is not going to change based on whether you use the word "bully" or "tease." What will help your child the most is helping him think through how to respond to the bully, which will then help him become less scared.

Parenting Behaviors That Increase Emotional Self-Awareness

You might think the above conversation seems too sophisticated for a six-year-old. Notice the artful way Juan's dad crafts the conversation. The dad does most of the work to help Juan develop emotional self-awareness. And, keep in mind that you and your child will need multiple discussions over the years just like any other skill you want your child to learn. Remember that EI is a skill that must be practiced just like soccer, the piano, or multiplication tables. One lesson would not allow the child to develop mastery in these other areas and neither will that happen with emotional intelligence skills.

Essential

Children model your actions. If you expect a child to identify her emotions when they occur, you must be able to identify your own emotions accurately. And you need to model discussing emotions.

Labeling Emotions

Talk about emotions using precise words such as mad (angry), sad, scared, embarrassed, excited, happy, and so on rather than using more generic words like "upset" all the time. The more precise the language, the easier it will be for kids to begin distinguishing the difference between "mad" and "scared," both of which could cause a child to feel "upset." So, master your use of emotion words! Notice that when dad first asked Juan how he felt, Juan said, "I don't know." At that point, it's fine for you to make an educated guess based on knowing your child and thinking about the information the child has already shared. Juan's dad ventured an educated guess that Juan was scared based on what he knew and that helped Juan acknowledge and label his emotion.

🅴❗ Alert

Children as young as one begin to learn emotion words so start using those words early with your child, just as you would words to label objects.

Based on temperament, modeling your actions, and past experiences, children are likely to experience emotions at different levels of intensity. For example, a child could be *terrified* of going to the doctor or *concerned* about it. Both emotions lie on a continuum of "fear" but they represent different intensity levels. The same is true of anger (irritated to fury), sadness (down to depressed or inconsolable), happiness (pleased to ecstatic), disgust (aversion to loathing), and embarrassed (uncomfortable to mortified or humiliated). Try to match your use of emotion words with the intensity of your child's behavior or words. Avoid, at all costs, using the most intense word when one with less intensity would be more appropriate. You don't want to intensify the emotion with your word choices!

Practice Understanding What Caused the Emotion

Emotions serve as a warning that something's not quite right or that something very good has happened. Teach your child to understand the cause of the emotion just as you would if your child had a stomachache and you knew she had eaten too much candy. Linking emotions to their root source or cause enables you to more effectively manage the emotion and your behavioral reaction to it.

Juan's warning system was alerting him that these kids were doing something hurtful to him and that they would have more opportunities on the bus. It's typical to be scared in this situation. You can help your child begin to understand the cause or source of an emotion by asking open-ended questions (e.g., What made you feel that way? or, What happened?). Or, you can take a more indirect approach by using story characters, asking your child to identify what emotion the character was feeling and what caused the feeling. Finally, you can remind the child about times he's seen you express emotion and then link that to the cause. "Remember that day I was so sad when I found out my friend has cancer?"

Practice Understanding an Emotion's Impact on Others

Again, one of the best ways to teach children to watch for the impact of emotions involves using concrete experiences. "Remember that day when you got mad at your sister and yelled at her? What did she do after you yelled at her?" Help your child make the connection between what he does and how that impacts others. Being aware of his emotional impact on others will make it less likely that your child will express emotions in a destructive or hurtful way or in a way that leaves him more vulnerable to others because they achieved the effect they wanted.

Many people use some form of "time out" as a discipline technique and it can also be used to build emotional intelligence. Time out involves asking a child sit quietly in a designated location after misbehavior so he has time to calm down and think about what he did. After two or three minutes, go to the child and ask the following questions, each of which helps build emotional self-awareness.

First ask the child what he did that was not appropriate. Let's say your four-year-old grabbed a toy from another child. Help your child identify the inappropriate behavior. Then ask your child why he did that. You'd be surprised at what children can articulate such as, "He wouldn't let me play with that toy." An effective response from you that will build emotional self-awareness might be, "That probably made you mad (or frustrated) because you like that toy so much." Identifying and labeling the emotion for the child will enable him to gain skill in this area such that he will automatically label the emotion in the future without you having to take the lead. Finally, ask the child what he could have done other than grab the toy from the other child. Closing the loop by identifying a more appropriate behavioral reaction to an emotion teaches your child that emotions don't have to control him; rather, he can choose how to react to emotions. Talk to your child about the consequences of different behaviors. Asking for the toy, suggesting a way to share the toy, or soliciting adult help for sharing would all make the other child more interested in playing with your child. Grabbing the toy, however, will have the impact of other kids avoiding your child and the sooner he recognizes this, the better.

CHAPTER 4

Self-Regard

Do you want your child to be confident but not cocky or arrogant? Do you want your child to want to improve when improvement is needed? Do you want your child to be able to say "I'm sorry" with authenticity? Do you want your child to recognize strengths and equally be able to identify her mistakes so she can fix them? Almost every parent would answer "yes" to each of these questions. Typically, parental motivation isn't the issue when it comes to developing children's self-regard; instead, it's misguided beliefs or efforts about how to help children build self-regard.

What Is Self-Regard?

Confusing, and sometimes contradictory, advice exists related to developing children's self-regard. Much of that advice uses different and sometimes confusing language—what is self-esteem? or self-confidence? or self-concept? or self-acceptance? And, how does each of those differ from the other? The term self-regard, as used in the Bar-On model of emotional intelligence described in Chapter 1, incorporates all of the above concepts. *Self-concept* refers to your ability to objectively analyze yourself. What do you do well? What do you struggle with? Self-concept makes up part one of self-regard and can best be described as **awareness** of strengths and limitations.

Self-esteem addresses whether you like and accept yourself the way you are, which is also sometimes called ***self-acceptance***. A child can have very high self-acceptance while also knowing he has skill or knowledge areas that must be improved; in fact, this combination is very healthy and appropriate for both adults and children!

⊜❗ Alert

Authentic self-regard—as opposed to cockiness or arrogance—is accompanied by a quiet confidence and willingness to acknowledge mistakes. If someone brags about accomplishments and never admits mistakes, they don't have authentically high self-regard.

Finally, *self-confidence* includes how confident, or not, a child feels about her ability to accomplish certain tasks or meet certain challenges. This confidence or ***attitude*** emerges directly from an accurate *awareness* of strengths and limitations as well as healthy *acceptance* because your child does not have to pretend that a skill exists or hide weaknesses. In fact, this confidence is further strengthened by the twin towers of self-acceptance and the desire for improvement.

Why Self-Regard?

Your child will face many challenges and the higher her self-regard, the more likely she will be to master those challenges, learn more about herself in the process, determine the valuable lessons within each, learn where she needs to improve, and prepare herself for the next big challenge with an attitude of confidence. After all, parents cannot be with their children every minute of every day so you must equip them with the skills to navigate the challenges they face. And, remember, high self-regard does not present as cockiness or arrogance; genuinely high self-regard typically presents as confident and humble.

 **Essential**

Adults and children above the age of six or seven with well-developed self-regard have less trouble apologizing when they're wrong. Why? Because they can be accepting of their limitations (some type of mistake that requires an apology) without losing confidence.

The Building Blocks of Self-Regard

Remember, self-regard includes three distinct but equally important components: accurate awareness of strengths and weaknesses, healthy self-acceptance as you are now but with a desire to improve weaknesses, and an attitude of confidence that stems from self-acceptance and self-respect, knowing what skills you possess as you face each new challenge.

Here's how healthy self-regard might sound coming from a child who is assessing his academic skills: "I'm a lot better at math than spelling (*awareness*), but that's okay because I'm working hard on my spelling (*acceptance with desire to improve*) and each time I do better, it helps me know I can become a good speller (*attitude of confidence*). Now I don't dread spelling tests."

Accurate Awareness of the Self

Young infants rapidly develop a sense of self in the first few months of life. One of the first outward indications you may see occurs when they discover their hands and feet. You probably remember your two-month-old child staring excitedly at her feet as she kicked them. "Those things belong to me," she may be thinking. Or, watch as an infant stares at his hand. "Me" is beginning to take shape; *physical self-awareness* has begun. Accurate awareness involves much more than your child understanding her physical attributes. It also involves her understanding things about her personality, her skills, and her interests.

Think of this part of self-regard (also known as self-concept in some literature) as an *accurate description of who you are*. Most three-year-olds can accurately describe physical characteristics such as "boy" with "brown hair" and so on. Older children add in characteristics such as height, weight, eye color, skin color, and so on without too much difficulty. Describing self moves from just the physical, to including categories such as "first grader" or "Girl Scout" or "sister" to the more advanced ability to describe other characteristics about themselves that are not as easy to quantify or categorize, such as what they like, their personality characteristics and skills.

 Essential

It's hard to remove all evaluative language when talking with children. So, if you hear an evaluative word slip out such as "You're such a *great* big brother," follow it up with descriptions of what the child did that was great such as, "You got your sister her pacifier when she started crying."

Focus on the words *"accurate awareness"* when thinking about self-concept. To help build your child's *accurate* self-concept, use descriptive language of what the child did rather than evaluating it. A descriptive sentence may sound like, "You worked on that math problem for twenty minutes. You were able to stick with it even after you got frustrated." This simple description will do far more to help a child gain a sense of self as "determined" or "persistent" than saying something like "You did a great job with your math homework; I'm so proud of you!" Describing behaviors enables the child to be more *aware* of how her behaviors contribute to the outcomes; and, the more aware she is of what worked in the past, the more likely she will be to repeat the behaviors the next time she encounters a big challenge.

So, what about weaknesses? Are you supposed to describe those too? Remember, part of self-regard involves recognizing areas that need improvement. *Observing* and *describing* behaviors helps a child identify those areas. And, if the observation is delivered in a neutral (non-judgmental) tone and with a calm voice, it provides a mirror to your child, helping him build *awareness of* his behavior. A descriptive sentence such as "I noticed you stopped working on that math problem the minute you got frustrated" helps your child see his behavior.

But, what should you do next? Keep observing. Maybe your child will try the problem again or maybe he'll ask for your help; both actions indicate a willingness to overcome at least one weakness (lack of persistence or underdeveloped math skills) and once again, *describe* the choice he made to keep working on something that's hard.

But, what if he doesn't open the math book? Again, describe what you see and help the child see possible consequences, "You've chosen not to work on your math anymore. What might happen in class tomorrow when the teacher collects math homework or asks you to work a problem for the class?"

🔔 Alert

Avoid the temptation to immediately fix your child's weaknesses such as a lack of persistence with homework. Stay neutral—this helps the child with self-acceptance and self-respect—describe what you've observed, and ask questions that will help the child figure out the possible consequences of his choice.

Self-Acceptance of Strengths and Weaknesses

Part two of self-regard involves self-esteem or whether you like, *accept*, and respect yourself as you are. Some (misguided) parenting advice over the last few decades has suggested that to build self-esteem, parents need to make kids feel good about themselves no matter what. A parent who follows such advice might end up praising work or effort even the child knows was not terrific. "You're a terrific artist" or, "You played better than anybody today even though you didn't score any goals," or "Your science project was the best and should have won first place" do *not* automatically build healthy self-acceptance. Ironically, the science project comment is sometimes muttered by a parent who did 75 percent of the real work on the project and the child knows it!

Less humorous is the impact of such behaviors and comments on the child. The child may be forming (or already playing) a mental tape that sounds like this, "Dad didn't think I could do the project, so he did most of it for me and now he's trying to make me feel better about it." Healthy self-acceptance would be more likely if the child had asked for help and the parents had restricted their help to showing the child how to do something and then letting the child do it; doing the work for the child erodes self-acceptance and sends a not-so-subtle message that weaknesses should be hidden not overcome.

Let's return to the child who is struggling with a math problem. How can you build self-acceptance without hurting confidence if a child is weak at a skill? First, make sure the skill or behavior is appropriate to the child's age or abilities. Giving a third-grade child a seventh-grade math problem is not appropriate unless the child is gifted in math. For now, though, assume the work assigned is appropriate for the child. When faced with obstacles or frustration, some children will give up; here's where you should step in. Ask your child if she'd like to learn how to solve that math problem.

You may think that's an unwise question because the child may say "no." Children want to succeed and they generally enjoy pleasing teachers and parents (most of the time, anyway!). So, a "no" answer can give you a clue that the child is avoiding her weaknesses perhaps out of fear of failure, fear of disappointing you, or some other reason. All of those reasons would point to a *lack of self-acceptance*. Whatever the reason, you must help your child understand that all people have strengths and weaknesses and that working to improve weaknesses is the only way to transform them into strengths. Tell your child a story about a time you kept working at something (e.g., learning a new software program, beginning a new sport, putting in extra effort in a weaker academic area when you were in school) and what happened as a result. Or, remind your child about a time when she remained persistent and experienced greater success as a result.

 **Question**

How much of your self-acceptance in your parent role depends on your child being the best or fastest or smartest?
When parental self-acceptance gets confounded with children's accomplishments, the inevitable result is that the parent creates too much pressure, communicates that weaknesses aren't tolerated, or inhibits the child's ability to gain accurate self-understanding. And, you're risking your own self-regard if you rely on your children's accomplishments to feed it!

Then, encourage your child to sit down and try that math problem again. Offer to help if the child asks for it, but do *not* do the work for the child. Doing the math problem for her will further deflate her self-acceptance ("I'm so bad at this Dad had to do it for me.") and self-confidence ("I won't be able to work the problem on the board if the teacher calls on me."). No one is perfect; it's counterproductive to children's self-regard to only acknowledge strengths and try to cover for weaknesses. What if your child still refuses to work on the math problem? Stick to any family rules about no TV or computer time until homework is finished and make it clear you stand ready to help her when she's ready. In other words, communicate that giving up is not okay; acknowledging weaknesses by working to improve them is expected.

 **Question**

> **Should I use the word "weakness" with my child?**
> Use whatever term you feel comfortable with—weakness, limitation, opportunity, improvement areas, and development areas are all choices—but be careful **not** to convey that weaknesses are bad. It won't be your word choice that conveys your attitude, it will be your ability to accept that your child does have weaknesses (and everyone does have weaknesses!).

Here's a story that may help. A children's book author was reading a draft of a story to a group of preschoolers to get their feedback. She asked her illustrator to come along so that they could do something fun with the kids after the reading, such as showing them how an artist draws an animal. One very astute child asked the author, "Why didn't you draw the pictures?" The author replied, "Because I can't draw." The teacher, who has a reputation for being a gifted facilitator of children's development then said to the author, "I think what you meant to say is that you're still learning to draw." Herein lies the heart of self-regard; it's healthy to know and accept your strengths and weaknesses; and, it's equally healthy to be determined to improve.

So what if your child does produce exceptional work? What should you say? Acknowledging exceptional work is fine, but focus on the process and the tangible outcomes more than evaluating the child. *Describing* what the child did is always appropriate. "You practiced stealing the ball all season and in today's soccer game, you stole the ball four times!" There's no reason to say "You're the best."

 Alert

Evaluative language is rampant. Listen to what you say. Do you use a lot of "great" or "terrific" or "best" or "awesome?" If so, practice describing more and evaluating less. Evaluative words don't help a child gain an accurate and objective sense of what one must do to be considered great or terrific.

A child who consistently hears himself described as the "best," "most gifted," "smartest," or "most popular" may exalt in his wonderfulness so much that he becomes cocky (which is different from confident) and forgets what behaviors made him popular, smart, or excellent. Authentic *self-acceptance* involves understanding both strengths and weaknesses and liking yourself as you are but with a goal to improve. Self-acceptance might sound like the following uttered by the nine-year-old soccer player who had mastered stealing the ball. "I stole the ball a lot today but when I tried to pass it, I didn't do as well. My coach said she would help me get better at passing. I'm going to ask for some drills."

Self-Confidence

Where does self-confidence fit when describing self-regard? Think of self-confidence as an attitude children develop when they know they have the skills or ability to accomplish something. And, when children accomplish something, they gain self-confidence naturally. Riding a bike without falling gives your daughter confidence to get on the bike the next day. Participating in the first dance recital or judo competition makes a child more confident for the next time. Scoring fairly high on a math test gives a child confidence to tackle tough math problems.

Remember, focusing on the process and on concrete behaviors (e.g., the child did all her homework, completed the review problems assigned by the teacher, and asked you to make up some more practice problems) allows her to better understand what she did that led to the positive outcomes. Plus, you are *describing behaviors* that are concrete; thus your child can picture those behaviors and repeat them. Generalized praise, "You did that so well" or evaluative statements, "You're a good artist" that aren't accompanied by descriptions about what the child did may ultimately *erode* self-regard. How can you build confidence if you don't understand what it was that you did well? How can you repeat the action if the action isn't described? And, if you're a "good" artist, you can also be a "bad" artist, a point that children quickly pick up.

Alert

Avoid doing things for a child that she can do for herself. You're robbing her of the chance to practice skills or behaviors that will develop confidence.

Or, even worse, think about the impact of praise that goes well beyond the accomplishment. When a child hears "You're a terrific soccer player" and everyone, including the child, knows that's an exaggeration, it can make the child less secure in his abilities. "Am I so bad that my parents have to tell me how great I am when they know I'm not great?" might be running through the child's head. And, as a reminder, if someone can be "terrific" at something, they can also be "horrendous" or "awful" as well. Your child might quickly jump to the conclusion that if he doesn't hear how "terrific" he was, he must have been "awful."

Self-Regard: Parenting Practices

So what can you do and say to help build self-regard? Lots! First, model the ability to engage in accurate self-awareness, healthy self-acceptance of strengths and limitations, a desire to improve, and confidence. When interacting with your child, remember to describe behaviors, celebrate accomplishments (but with language that helps the child know how to repeat the success), and talk about how to improve weaknesses. Support the child's efforts to improve by teaching her skills, but don't do the work for her.

Consider this conversation between ten-year-old Natasha and her mother before a big tennis match. Notice the change in the child's attitude as the conversation progresses.

Natasha (tearful): I'm scared I'm going to mess up today. The coaches are counting on me to win my match.

Mom (with a gentle hand on Natasha's shoulder): You're feeling lots of pressure because of what the coach told you.

Natasha: Yeah.

Mom: Let's think about what you've practiced this summer. You did lots of practice serving the ball. And, you practiced your returns every day. *(accurately describe behaviors)*

Natasha: I know, but I'm still scared.

Mom: I'm sure you are. This is a big match. You've come a long way this summer. At the beginning of the summer, you were having trouble getting your serves in (modeling *acceptance of weaknesses)* and now you've played your last three matches without double faulting. *(accurately describe behaviors; acknowledging improvement)*

Natasha: And, I stayed after practice to get the coach to help me with my serve so I could get better. *(acceptance of weaknesses, desire to improve)*

Mom: And, I think I saw you practicing your service returns too. *(accurately describing behavior; accepting of current behavior with desire to improve)*

Natasha: Yeah, and the coach even counted how many I got back and I've gone from 50 percent to 80 percent. I feel a lot better about that! *(attitude of confidence)*

Mom: That's great! I'm excited for you.

Natasha: I'm still nervous because I want to win my match.

Mom: Sure you do, winning is fun. No matter what happens though, you have improved a lot this summer and can get even better at tennis in the future if you keep working at it. *(modeling acceptance and attitude of confidence)*

✅ Fact

Expect children to experience some anxiety before a big competition, test, or event that is important to them. A moderate level of anxiety actually helps people perform better. Those who don't get anxious at all may not care enough to do their best and those who get too anxious are often too distressed to perform well. So, don't try to talk children out of their anxiety!

The conversation between Natasha and her mom could have become derailed in multiple places; consider some of the responses below and think about whether they would build healthy self-regard. All of the responses are well intentioned to ease the child's anxiety, but that doesn't make them helpful; nor do they build emotional intelligence.

Natasha (tearful): I'm scared I'm going to mess up today. The coaches are counting on me to win my match.

Mom: I know you can do it. You're a great tennis player! (This is an attempt to build confidence but "great" isn't specific enough.)

Natasha: But, I've had trouble with my serve.

Mom: Yeah, but you've worked really hard lately and gotten so much better. (The words "hard" and "better" aren't specific enough to be helpful. What behaviors could the mother describe? Also, could she acknowledge the self-acceptance of a weakness and desire to improve?)

Natasha: But what if I don't win?

Mom: Well, we'll talk about that if it happens. All you should think about now is how good you've become. (This is an attempt to build *confidence* but it's not grounded in any of Natasha's behaviors.)

Natasha: But some of the other players are good too. (Notice the child isn't comforted or made more confident by broad, evaluative terms of praise.)

Mom: That's right, so you'll just have to give it your best effort. (What does "best effort" mean in terms of behaviors? Can you give your best effort and still lose? This attempt to motivate Natasha may make her more anxious.)

The second conversation deprives Natasha of opportunities to understand what she has done to improve and how she can become more confident. Natasha's self-acceptance of her limitations as a tennis player and desire to improve go almost unnoticed and instead, the focus is on thinking about winning.

Remember the three "As" when you're working to build healthy self-regard in your children: accurate self-*awareness,* healthy self-*acceptance* of strengths and weaknesses (which is accompanied by a desire to improve), and *an attitude* of confidence that results from knowing one's strengths and limits, working to improve, and being confident that improvement will happen.

CHAPTER 5

Self-Actualization

Self-actualization sounds like a lofty principle for a child of any age, much less one who is ten or younger. Yet, self-actualization applies very well to children, even those in preschool. If you hear your five-year-old say she "loves painting," or your seven-year-old talks about adopting a homeless pet so it will have a good home, or your nine-year-old talks about wanting to be the best gymnast she can be, then you are hearing statements that reflect self-actualization.

What Is Self-Actualization?

If you want your child to pursue things she loves doing, receive satisfaction from those activities, and learn to set goals about her participation or performance, then you are endorsing self-actualization. So, don't get tied down with the loftiness of the word. Instead, think about goals (appropriate to the child's age) or purpose, and the meaning, satisfaction, and joy that come through activities your child loves to do.

Why Is Self-Actualization Important?

You might be thinking, "But why should a five-year-old need purpose? Shouldn't he just enjoy being a kid?" Absolutely, yes! Purpose doesn't mean, however, that you have to take the fun out of life or out of play. Rather, purpose can sometimes add fun. Building a sand castle at the beach, making a craft for Mother's or Father's Day, or learning to ride a bike all involve purposeful activity. When children engage in such activity, typically they enjoy (or at least learn from) the process and feel some sense of accomplishment and happiness when they see the final product or achieve the goal. Others may share the joy and thus reinforce the behavior of hard work (practicing fine motor skills involved in art), taking a risk (falling several times when learning to balance on the bike) or even persistence (rebuilding part of your sand castle when someone accidentally steps on it).

 Fact

Infants show purposeful activity when they do something such as stick a pacifier in their mouth, pull on a blanket so that a toy can be reached, and a myriad of other behaviors. "Goal setting" begins early!

Learning to set goals—whether it's riding a bike without falling, reading your first book by yourself, or going to sleep without a light on—teaches children to think about ways to stretch themselves, gain new skills, or accomplish something important. They'll need these goal setting abilities for the rest of their lives whether in school (e.g., completing a degree), at work (e.g., getting a promotion), or in their personal lives (e.g., saving money for a house). So, don't think of goal setting, achievement, or purpose as topics that are too serious for children. Instead, help them recognize the many ways they are naturally setting goals and the joy they are receiving when a goal is accomplished.

An Example of Self-Actualization

This example about a seven-year-old may help. Matthew loved to play in the pool but did not know how to swim and had not been interested in taking lessons. One day he went to the neighborhood pool with the twins who lived next door. As it turned out, the pool was holding tryouts for their summer swim team, the Woodcroft Whirlwinds. This was a very popular summer activity and the team frequently won the city championship. The twins from next door had no problem meeting the requirement to swim twenty-five yards without holding the lane line or touching the bottom. Matthew desperately wanted to join the twins and his other friends on the swim team. He asked if he could try out.

Although a non-swimmer, Matthew was determined to make the swim team. So, he dog-paddled his way twenty-five yards without touching the bottom or holding onto the lane line. The achievement is even more amazing because he paused every three or four yards to wipe the water from his face, a sensation that had kept him from wanting to learn to swim!

Talk about setting a goal—this child identified something important to him, and fueled by determination and courage, he achieved it. He exited the pool breathing hard but beaming at his accomplishment. He couldn't wait to share the news with everyone! His stunned parents knew that supporting his effort was the only sensible thing to do, so they paid the fee to join the swim team. Even though Matthew jumped off the starting block instead of diving and frequently wiped his face during most of his races, he gradually improved.

By the summer he was eight, he was awarded the "most improved" swimmer and by ten, he was named the "most valuable" swimmer for his age group. He began to win races, joined a year-round swim team, and set a goal to swim at the highest level (Division I NCAA) in college. He earned that swimming scholarship and at one point held a top ten fastest time at his university.

Seven-year-old Matthew set a goal, achieved it, and experienced years of satisfaction and joy as a result. And, he received other benefits as well. He learned that sometimes accomplishments come with great effort (grueling practices) and some sacrifices (getting up at 5:00 A.M. to swim before school every morning of his high school career). In other words, he learned about priorities, discipline, and effort, things that helped him graduate with honors from college while also competing as an athlete.

 **Question**

Do you think Matthew would have become an elite swimmer if his parents had forced him to join the swim team? More important, do you think Matthew would have enjoyed swimming, gaining the same level of satisfaction, achievement, and drive as he did if forced by his parents to begin swimming before he was ready?
The answer is a resounding no. Allow, support, and encourage children, but try to avoid forcing things onto your child. Force just doesn't yield the same positive results.

Children and Goal Setting: Yours, Theirs, or Both?

Most people have witnessed the overly zealous parent standing on the sidelines of a soccer game, urging his child to compete harder, run faster, kick the ball straighter, and so on. Parents, it's your responsibility to help your child understand the importance of goals and achievements, but it is *not* wise for you to set goals for the child. Is the child on the soccer field typically more or less motivated with a parent shouting from the sideline, hovering around at practices, insisting on extra practice in the back yard, and so on? You know the answer.

✅ Fact

Abraham Maslow, a famous humanistic psychologist, used the term self-actualization a bit differently from how the term is used in the EQi model, but both definitions include finding meaning and fulfillment. Maslow focused more on inward peace, whereas the Bar-On model focuses on goal setting, accomplishment of goals, and the joy derived from that.

Basically, there are three ways that children can get involved in activities. The first model involves the parent picking an activity that the child ends up enjoying and the child wants to continue to participate in the activity (mutually chosen). In the second model, the parent picks an activity the child does not want to participate in and the child is forced to participate (parent chosen). In the third model, the child finds activities that challenge and satisfy him that the parents then support (child chosen). Matthew and swimming fit the last category.

A Word about Intrinsic and Extrinsic Motivation

Before examining the impact of mutually chosen, parent-chosen, and child-chosen activities, consider the distinction between intrinsic and extrinsic motivation. *Intrinsic motivation* comes from within and propels children (adults too) to work hard on pursuits because they enjoy the activity itself and what they gain from participating. No one has to entice, cajole, or reward participation. Participating brings joy and satisfaction and that fuels continued involvement.

Contrast intrinsic motivation with *extrinsic motivation*, which involves providing some type of external incentive or reward for doing something or accomplishing a goal. Money or extra TV or computer time earned for good grades, getting a goal in the soccer game, or earning badges in scouts are all examples of extrinsic motivation. Extrinsic motivation works well in situations that are challenging for the child but will become easy and expected with no need for reward once the activity is mastered (think potty training!).

 **Essential**

> If you are going to use extrinsic motivators, try to always make them something positive the child can earn rather than something negative that will happen if the child doesn't perform. And make sure you pick things your child finds rewarding, not things you think she would enjoy or that are convenient for you.

Extrinsic motivation often fails when it comes to children's participation in activities that are required of them (school) or that they already enjoy. Why? Simply put, we are teaching the child that the external reward is more important than the internal satisfaction and joy savored by the participation and the sense of accomplishment. Psychologists call this the *overjustification effect*—in other words, too many external incentives can squelch internal passion. You're "overjustifying" the child's effort when it's not needed.

Take the example of second-grader Emily. Emily and her parents had a nightly ritual of reading two books before bed time, one read aloud by Emily to her parents and the other read to Emily. Emily loved this nighttime reading ritual, but one night early in the month of September she announced to her mother that she didn't need to read that night. Why not, inquired her mother? Well, it seems as if Emily's school had begun an incentive program; if a child read at least fifteen books that month, she got a reward. Ironically, the award was for $3 off a pizza at a local pizza parlor. So, even though the reward didn't directly benefit Emily—after all, she didn't pay for the pizza—the mere fact that it was offered as a reward reduced her intrinsic desire to read. She had met the quota to receive the reward (extrinsic motivation) and thereby lost some of her passion for reading (intrinsic motivation). Needless to say, Emily's mom visited the school. She suggested they introduce an additional strategy of encouraging the kids to write in a journal each morning about a book they read the night before. The next night, Emily's passion for reading burned brightly again.

Mutually Chosen Activities: Parent and Child Agree

Mutually chosen activities are those that the parent may at first select for the child—signing her up for Girl Scouts, t-ball, or gymnastics—and then the child embraces the activity with joy. The parents, in effect, picked something that matched their child's temperament, talents, and interests. The child participates with gusto and looks forward to the activity. All is well.

But, not always. If the parents take on the role of support and encouragement and leave the instruction and goal setting to the child and leaders, then harmony reigns. The child will most likely set her own goals to earn badges, get hits in the game, or something else. Parents can inquire about goals, but if a child senses excessive demands for achievement or feels too much pressure, she will often push back. Or, worse, she will go through the motions to please the parents, even while becoming more and more disenchanted with the activity because there's too much pressure.

Your insistence on additional practice, higher and higher goals, and other forms of demands may rob her of her joy for the activity. Or, she'll actively rebel and arguments about whether she can quit will begin to pop up. So, if an activity resonates with your child, let her develop naturally and at her own pace.

But what are you supposed to do if your child isn't inclined to earn the badges in Girl Scouts or doesn't want to practice doing cartwheels, or spend time at the piano? Isn't it right for the parents to set expectations for the child? After all, the parent is spending precious time and money to support the child's involvement and the child has made a commitment to participate. Here's a simple rule of thumb: In almost every case, if your child really enjoys the activity (that is, gets meaning, satisfaction, and purpose from it), she would be motivated to earn the badges, practice her skills or do whatever it takes to fully participate because it's satisfying to her.

 Alert

You'll be able to tell if you're the one setting goals or pushing too hard for the child to set goals when he stops wanting to talk with you about the activity.

Suppose that's what the coach or leader reports when you inquire about her participation during meetings or in practice. In other words, when the leader or coach is in charge, she's motivated and engaged. It's only when you step in and push for that extra achievement that she loses interest. Take your cue. If you relax, her natural enjoyment and goal setting will be allowed to flourish. Remember the non-swimmer Matthew? He had no idea when he was ten or twelve that he wanted to become a college swimmer. But, he did know he wanted to get faster and win races and so he practiced diligently. Other goals materialized as he grew in the sport.

Parent-Chosen Activities

Well-intentioned parents enroll their children in a myriad of activities between the ages of five and ten, searching for one or two that fit their child. That's effective parenting; after all, you don't know what your child may love until he gives it a try. But, what if he doesn't like an activity you've chosen for him? Should you let him quit? Aren't there important lessons to be learned from sticking with an activity until completion?

Suppose both parents are very artistic, one with a career as an artist and the other as a photographer. You enroll your son in art and photography classes, piano lessons, and drama camp. Nothing excites him. He resists going. Your son begins to balk at each new activity. At age eight, he begs to join the local soccer team. You and your spouse are not athletic and have no interest standing on a sideline in the hot sun and watching soccer. So, you find a different type of artistic activity, guitar lessons. You promise to buy him a guitar if he sticks with it for six months, convinced that if he just gives it a try, things will work well. After two months, he's begging to quit guitar lessons. He cares nothing about earning a guitar. So, you tell him that if he sticks with it for six months, he can play soccer next year. Next year is too long for an eight-year-old to wait. So, the battle continues.

Decisions to let a child quit an activity can be simple ones. First, before a child begins an activity, talk to your child about the importance of commitments. (This will work though only if the child is given a choice about participating. If he's being forced, then the commitment discussion is a moot point.) If he's on a team and the team needs ten players, the whole team suffers if he quits. Before enrolling a child in any activity, let him know the activity's duration and your expectation for how long he must stick with the activity (end of the season, until Thanksgiving, etc.), even if he decides he doesn't like it.

And, before you let a child quit, talk to your child about giving an activity a reasonable chance. Matthew's motivation to join the swim team was not born out of a love for swimming laps or learning strokes, rather it was fueled by a desire to be with friends. But, as he improved, he began to enjoy the sport because he got faster and felt more confident about what he was doing.

But what if your child wants to quit an activity you selected that he really dislikes? Let's suppose you chose the activity, announced his participation to him with no discussion or a discussion dominated by you explaining why this is a good activity for him. And, let's say your child is not only disinterested in the activity, but unskilled at it compared with the performance of other kids. He's miserable and likely embarrassed in front of his peers. In this circumstance, engage in problem solving with the child. Will anything make the activity more interesting or better for your child? What does he want to do instead of the activity you chose? Remember, if your goal is to help your child find meaningful activities that bring joy to his life, continuing something you chose that he hates accomplishes none of this. Let the child quit as long as his withdrawal does not jeopardize other children's participation (e.g., not enough kids on the team). Follow that with a discussion about what activities the child wants to do and the commitments he needs to make to the activity he picks.

ⓔ⚠ Alert

Examine your attitudes about quitting something and how they were developed. Remember, there are only a few reasons children ask to quit—embarrassment about skill level, disinterest or dislike (who chose the activity, you or them?), or something going wrong such as a harsh coach. Find out why your child wants to quit. Don't just automatically say "no."

A story may help to understand this. Marie's mother was convinced that taking piano lessons was important. Without consulting her daughter, she signed Marie up for the lessons. Luckily, Marie enjoyed the lesson time with the teacher. But, she didn't like the thirty minutes of practice she was required to do as a seven-year-old beginning player. The practice did pay off, and by the end of two years, Marie was one year ahead of most other kids her age who had taken piano for two years. Marie still didn't love to practice, but she loved her teacher and enjoyed improving.

Then Marie's teacher retired. Marie's mom found a new instructor, one who was more critical, more demanding, and less warm.

Marie dreaded going to lessons and began to really balk at the practice time required. She began asking to quit. Her mother refused, citing her wonderful progress and that Marie needed to learn to adjust to different styles and different people. Over a three-year period, with multiple tearful pleadings, and lots of conflict about practice time, Marie trudged through because she wasn't allowed to quit. Finally, her mother gave in. After five years, three with this new teacher, Marie was stuck at the same level of mastery that she had accomplished in just two years with the first teacher.

Marie's mother apologized to her as an adult, noting that she should have let Marie quit sooner. Instead of seeing Marie's push back as a sign of legitimate unhappiness, she viewed it as disobedience and held her ground. And, she didn't want Marie to think that she, as the child, was in control of important decisions. The core issue here was not disobedience (she did practice) or control over decisions; rather, the core issue is that Marie was forced to participate in something that brought her no joy or satisfaction, and thus her performance lagged significantly.

You may be able to force an activity on a child, but you cannot force her to love it or perform well. That comes from her intrinsic motivation and when that's missing, the activity is tolerated at best and becomes a lightning rod for discontent and rebellion at worst.

Child-Chosen Activities

Remember Matthew? He chose swimming, a sport his parents would have never considered signing him up for because he could not swim! They had tried soccer and t-ball and neither of those sports were good fits for their son. They enrolled him in Boy Scouts and piano lessons. Although he attended both with no complaints, he wasn't energized by either, not wanting to build a go-kart, go on the camping trips, practice, or participate in recitals.

His parents were going through activities rapidly, even considering a chess club, when Matthew himself discovered swimming. Sometimes, the very best thing parents can do to support children's learning and development is to follow their child! If parents listen and observe, children will provide a road map. Their interests will emerge and if engaged in what they love, goals will be accomplished, satisfaction present, and joy in the process evident.

 **Question**

What if I don't enjoy an activity my child has chosen and wants to continue?
Your support means a lot to your child. Think about what you're modeling with your decision to support or not support the activity. And, being supportive does not mean you have to attend every game or performance, but you do need to attend at least some of the time.

What about School: Who Sets the Goals?

Reread the header. The answer to the question should be—the child. Gulp. Are you really supposed to stand by and let a child under-perform in school? No, you're not. If a child is under-performing, and the reason is related to effort or commitment, there should be consequences such as no TV time or cell phone. Under-performance though, is a far cry from goal setting by parents that includes a child making all As or reaching some other very high standard.

The message is simple: Set your expectations about work ethic (effort) and work quality and grades will take care of themselves. If the child violates the expectations about effort or quality, he will suffer the consequences of worse grades. Constant pressure to achieve all As or a certain GPA can interfere with children's learning. Remember the overjustification effect? Applying too much extrinsic motivation related to *grades* (consequences for bad grades, rewards for good grades) will likely rob the child of the joy and satisfaction of achievement. Learning is fun; producing high-quality work is satisfying and accomplishing a goal is energizing. Let those naturally occurring responses be the impetus for learning.

❗ Alert

Be careful how you handle rewarding grades in your family, especially if you have one child with special needs such as a learning disability and others who don't have a learning disability. It may be unreasonable to expect the same grades. Effort, however, can be expected from everyone.

You can and should set expectations about effort, follow-through, or work quality. By doing so, you'll help your child learn lessons about work ethic, responsibility, and accomplishment. Here's an example. During the summer months, Lamar's mom set an expectation that he should read one book a week. At first, there was an extrinsic reward because Lamar did not like to read. What he read was up to him as long as it was a certain number of pages. When he inquired about reading *Sports Illustrated*, his mom agreed and took him weekly to the local library. Very quickly, the extrinsic reward (more computer time) faded. In fact, he became so engrossed in reading about sports that it was easy to keep a stack of biographies about famous athletes readily available.

 **Question**

What should a parent do if the child asks to be paid for good grades?
Answer the child by asking a question—why does she want to be paid? Maybe it's because friends are paid or maybe she wants more spending money. There's not an absolute right answer to this question. Just make sure your answer meets two criteria: first, her intrinsic motivation stays strong, and second, that you are supporting and encouraging her to achieve goals important to her.

What about work quality? Set goals there also, as long as the goal is about quality, not the final grade. Consider this example. Kate was a fourth grader who excelled in math. Spelling, however, was very difficult for her and the weekly spelling test spiked her anxiety. The quality rule her parents set was that she would practice the twenty-word list until she could get seventeen of the twenty correct at home. Sometimes this took over twenty minutes a night during the week. Often, Kate wanted to continue until she could spell all twenty words correct (intrinsic motivation). On test day, Kate sometimes got all the words correct but typically misspelled three or four of them, often earning a B instead of an A. But her effort was good, she was improving, and she was responding well to the guidelines set for her.

CHAPTER 6

Emotional Expression

"Big boys don't cry" is a phrase most of us have heard or maybe even delivered at some time. But is that a wise thing to say? Does trying to suppress emotional expression (you cannot suppress the emotion itself) help children become stronger or does it erode their ability to be genuine, self-accepting, and connected to others? All humans experience multiple emotions every day. Emotions come seeping out in our behavior and through nonverbal cues. It's both more honest and healthier to also express them verbally.

What Does Emotional Expression Involve?

Humans express emotions in two ways, verbally and nonverbally. Nonverbal expression of emotions, which typically accounts for over 90 percent of total emotional expression, includes eye contact, facial expressions, tone of voice, body posture, gestures, and behaviors such as hitting or hugging. Verbal emotional expression includes seven basic emotions, including happiness, surprise, anger, fear, sadness, frustration, and disgust. Other emotion words, such as excited, hurt, or annoyed represent different intensity levels of the basic seven emotions. So, while rage would reflect the most intense degree of anger, annoyed would represent a much less intense level.

Ideally, emotional expression is congruent; in other words, your words match your nonverbal cues. But that doesn't always happen. In fact, many people avoid any verbal expression of emotion while obviously posturing with nonverbal cues. The person who replies "nothing" to your question of, "What's wrong?" but does so in an irritated voice, and with a frown and arms folded, clearly does have something wrong. In fact, he wants you to know something is wrong or he'd do a better job of hiding it.

🔔 Alert

Before you delve too far in this chapter, think about what messages your family gave you about *verbal* emotional expression. Was it allowed or forbidden? Were certain emotions okay but not others? It's important to actively choose what you want to teach your children about emotional expression and not just repeat what happened with your parents.

So, why won't that person say "I'm mad because . . ."? Probably because most children are expressly taught not to verbalize their emotions or they watch the grown-ups in their world avoid verbal expression while readily signaling with nonverbal cues such as a frown or irritated voice. Or, the child did express emotions verbally such as "I'm scared of that dog" or "I'm mad at my coach because I didn't get to play more" only to have an adult respond with "You shouldn't be scared of dogs, they won't hurt you" or "There are lots of good players on your team." Even though your intentions would be good in both cases, you've inadvertently told your child that his feelings are not warranted, suppressing his desire to express emotions to you in the future. Unfortunately though, not expressing the emotion does not dissipate it; instead, it will flow out through nonverbal expressions. Simply put, emotions don't work like a light switch that you can turn on or off. Once triggered, they are "on" and need to be expressed and managed appropriately.

Why Is Emotional Expression Important?

As discussed in Chapter 3, humans are wired to experience emotions, so to suppress them, you have to work against your natural biology. Human survival depends on emotion—that's what creates the fear to motivate you to get out of the way of an oncoming car—and thus emotion is first triggered in a more primitive part of the brain. The helpless human infant could not survive without its ability to generate powerful feelings of joy in others, leading adults to nurture the infant by providing for its basic needs, comforting it when distressed, and cuddling or playing with the infant.

Humans are also wired to react to threats—whether it's that oncoming car or someone who screams at you—by either "fighting" (honking your horn, yelling back) or "fleeing" by dropping way behind the erratic driver or leaving the room so the person can no longer yell at you.

The human infant has no way to communicate during the first few months of life except by crying, and then by three or four weeks after birth, by smiling. An infant's crying and smiling call adults to action, relieving the distress of an empty stomach or hot clothing on the one hand and ensuring adult love and attention on the other hand. From the beginning of life, emotional expression plays a key role in helping humans regulate their world and get their needs met.

The benefits of self-regulation and meeting needs to stay safe and be loved do not end just because you learn to walk and talk. In fact, it's precisely the development of speech that ensures you have an additional way to communicate.

Stifling verbal expression of emotion makes it more challenging for a child to self-regulate, or manage her behavior. Consider the child who is scared of dogs. Being told not to be scared doesn't remove the fear even though most dogs are harmless. What does remove the fear is an adult who hears that statement and patiently guides the child toward a greater comfort level by introducing a dog slowly, modeling a lack of fear, and allowing the child to progress at her own rate, perhaps watching from a distance, then approaching the dog, then patting the dog on the back (a dog's back has no teeth!), and so on. This lucky child has a loving adult who allowed the expression of fear and then helped the child conquer it. The child who is simply told not to be scared (or at least not to say that she's scared to that adult), does not conquer her fear. She just learns to suppress it as much as possible in front of that adult. Typically, though, the next time the child is near a dog, the nonverbal signs of fear will be very evident (e.g., standing far back, grabbing an adult's hand) even though the child may not say, "I'm scared."

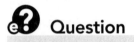 **Question**

Should parents respond to a crying infant?
Yes, every time for at least the first six months. It's impossible to "spoil" a child who doesn't know you exist except when she can see or hear you. When she cries, she's crying out of discomfort not because she knows "mommy will come." The concept of mommy doesn't exist yet. Crying is an infant's way of saying "help me" and the adult's job is to help!

Which child is better equipped to handle fear as she ages? Which child has learned to pay attention to her emotions? Which child has learned the lesson that if she communicates verbally about her emotions, others will help her deal with them in effective ways? Which child will be more likely to grow into an adult who can handle the emotions of a tough conversation, the disappointments she experiences, the inevitable ups and downs of family relationships, or the angry coworker? You know the answer; the one that has practiced expressing emotion authentically and had adults guide her effectively about how to handle those emotions. Her practice throughout life has primed her to express her emotions as an adult, understand how to cope with her emotions, and to be comfortable with others' emotions as well.

 **Essential**

Children's fears go through predictable stages; first it's separation from attachment figures, then it's concrete things they can hear or see like thunder or a dog, then, as their ability to imagine grows, they become afraid of monsters and ghosts. By late elementary school, they are more afraid of things they may hear about on TV such as war, being abducted, or similar fates that are unlikely but nevertheless terrifying to think about.

Teaching Emotional Expression

Teaching a child to express emotions freely is usually not a challenge. It's the *appropriate expression* of emotion that takes lots of guidance and patience. When children throw a temper tantrum, it's because they're mad and don't know another way to express it. How you react to a tantrum determines whether and how well a child will learn alternatives. Your goal is always to teach acceptable ways to express emotions verbally and nonverbally.

Label Feelings

How do children learn new vocabulary words? Typically, a person points to something and gives it a name (dog, car, ball, etc.) and the child tries to mimic the word. Or, sometimes children pick up words by watching or listening even when you're not teaching them directly. (There's a lesson here—be careful what you say!) The lesson is simple: label things you want them to learn and talk to them frequently. And, label your emotions, especially when talking with them. It's healthy for them to see you express anger or fear or sadness and explain why.

Most parents quickly learn the difference between their baby's hungry cry, tired cry, or mad cry and respond differently depending on which cry they hear. It's never too early to label the emotion the infant is expressing. The ten-month-old infant who is mad after being left alone too long in the crib cannot say the word "mad" but can begin to associate that word with a certain type of feeling.

✅ Fact

It's commonly understood that more of our emotional expression occurs nonverbally (typically over 90 percent) than verbally (using words such as mad or sad), leaving others to react to nonverbal cues they may have misinterpreted. No wonder there are so many misunderstandings!

As kids get older, it's even easier. They'll experience a full gamut of feelings throughout the day and your job is to help them express those appropriately. To the two-year-old who resists a nap because that means giving up play, it's appropriate to say "You're frustrated that you can't keep playing right now." To the five-year-old who expresses a fear of the dark, you can say "I'm glad you told me the dark scares you. What will help you be less scared?" To the eight-year-old who just had a pet cat die, you can say, "You're really sad that Tubby died. He was a good friend to you and you'll miss him." Or, to the ten-year-old who spilled milk all over her clothes at lunch time and was made fun of by friends at school, you can say, "That hurts when your friends tease you so much."

The learning is simple, calm, and neutral—there's no big deal about labeling emotion words any more than there would be naming a TV program. You're both helping the child understand which feelings she's experiencing and modeling how to talk about those feelings. The final step is to help her learn what to do with these emotions.

ⓔ Question

What are the consequences of labeling an emotion incorrectly? For example, what if a parent believes a child is mad, but what she's really feeling is sad?
Typically, a child will correct you if you incorrectly surmise which emotion she's feeling. The anger that you thought you observed about not being invited to a birthday party may really be sadness. She'll tell you or you'll pick up nonverbal cues that will guide you.

Allow Children to Have Their Feelings

You've probably had the experience of sitting in a room with another adult and one of you says, "It's cold in here" and the other replies, "No it's not. I'm a little hot." People can legitimately view the same thing in very different ways. The same thing can and does occur with feelings. Things that have never scared you may scare your child. Things that make you angry may not bother your child. Emotions and what triggers them are unique to each person. Be sure to allow your child to have her emotions.

Suppose your child seems to have a low frustration tolerance and that concerns you; do you try to talk the child out of the frustration or help him deal with it? Or, your child expresses anger about something (perhaps a newborn sibling) and the anger scares you, so you try to diminish the anger by saying things like, "You know you love your little sister. Be nice to her." The chances are that your child does not yet love her little sister and may in fact resent the loss of time with you or change in family routines. The attempt to talk the child out of her feelings will be likely to fortify her anger and to lessen her trust in you as someone she can count on to be accepting of her feelings. And, remember, accepting their feelings does not give children the freedom to misbehave. Don't assume that if you acknowledge their feelings they'll become tyrants. That won't happen if you also teach them how to appropriately manage these feelings.

Here's a true story that should help. One evening three-year-old Sam and his parents and two-month-old baby brother were invited to a friend's house. Before dinner, the dad played games like hide and seek with Sam and the neighbor's child. During dinner, Sam's dad talked to him, helped him with his food, and generally paid a lot of attention to him.

Alert

Sometimes when you listen to someone else's feelings, it can be difficult for you. It's hard to know your child is hurting, scared, or something else because that can create intense feelings in you. So, brace yourself so that you can be a good listener. And then, talk with your partner, a best friend, or someone else about the emotions you're having.

Just before it was time to leave, baby Charlie woke up. Dad immediately began attending to Charlie's wet diaper while mom gathered up their coats. Sam walked over to his father and asked, "Dad, can we drop Charlie off at the hospital on the way home? That's where we got him, right?" The father turned to face Sam and said, "Sam, you don't like your little brother very much right now, do you?" Sam just listened. His dad continued, "Well, I understand that because before he was born, you and I had lots more time together to play and read. Now, I spend some of my time playing with Charlie and taking care of him." Sam nodded, his eyes filling with tears. Dad continued, "Sam, I love you and I love Charlie, so we're not going to give either one of you away." Then the father reached out and gave Sam a huge hug. Sam beamed. His anger and jealousy didn't get him in trouble. In fact, expressing his anger openly was validated by his father's reply. His anger began to dissipate and he joyfully hugged his father.

Acknowledging feelings is the best way to help a child manage them. Trying to ignore or erase the child's feeling in hopes that it will go away almost never works.

The Art of an "I" Message

One simple strategy for expressing emotions involves teaching kids to use "I" messages. "I" messages have a simple formula. I feel (insert emotion) because (describe what someone else did to upset you). So, a five-year-old may say to a friend, "I'm mad because you took my toy."

Or, a three-year-old may say, "I'm sad. I miss Mommy" when the mom has gone out of town on business. A nine-year-old who doesn't want to swim in the ocean might say, "I'm scared that I'll get bitten by a crab." As you can see, each of these messages is clear and appropriate. And, "I" messages allow the child to express an emotion without becoming dramatic or falling apart.

The more everyone in your family uses "I" messages to express feelings, the more quickly the child will learn.

Managing Behaviors:
Give Kids Outlets for Their Feelings

Okay, you've labeled the child's feelings and maybe she can even express her emotions effectively verbally by saying things like "I'm mad." But what is she supposed to do with her anger after she's let you know she's mad and you've acknowledged the anger? Sometimes well-meaning adults squelch children's feelings because they have no idea how to help the child manage the feeling. There are numerous strategies for helping; all of them start with labeling the feeling and then accepting that as the child's emotion. You must also develop an array of options for kids to express their feelings in *appropriate nonverbal* ways.

Dealing with Anger

Depending on the age of the child, appropriate ways to manage anger could include anything from drawing a picture of what made the child mad (the adult equivalent of crafting an e-mail retort but without sending it), retreating to a special place to read books and calm down (have a name for this space and keep it off limits at other times), going outside to kick a soccer ball, or listening to music. After she's calmed down enough to problem solve, then you can talk about what other actions, if any, need to occur.

 Question

What should I do about temper tantrums?
If you are in a public setting, calmly remove the child to your car or back to your house. While this can be inconvenient, removing the child communicates that his behavior is not appropriate. And, you won't feel pressured to give in to keep the child quiet. If you're at home, you can let the tantrum play out by ignoring it. When your child is finished, ask why she was so mad. In other words, don't give the child attention until she completes the tantrum.

One more thing about anger: It's okay for kids to be mad with adults including teachers, coaches, and parents. Telling your child that it's not appropriate to be angry at an authority figure sends a confusing message to your child. Why are adults off limits? Does an adult never make a mistake? What most parents probably intend to communicate is that even when angry, kids need to be respectful and appropriate. That rule should apply to all people regardless of age, sex, nationality, or anything else.

Expressing Sadness

Sadness is an emotion that children experience frequently. Grandparents leaving to go home after an extended visit, mom or dad being away on business, a favorite animal dying, a lost toy or comfort object, or even something on a TV show can evoke sadness. Adults are tempted to "make it better" by offering an array of inducements to cheer the child up, whether it's a trip to the ice cream store, staying up late to watch a movie, or buying a new toy.

What's wrong with sadness? Why do we want to remove its sting? The answer is simple: seeing children sad probably makes most adults who care about them sad. Removing the sadness by inducements or extra privileges makes everyone feel better. But, it robs children of the opportunity to learn how to cope with sadness. Instead of a trip to the ice cream store, make up a story about a child who was sad and how he coped. Or, tell children about a time you were sad and what you did. Or, ask them to think of things that will make them feel better that acknowledge the feeling rather than eradicate it. For example, a young child could dictate a letter to the grandparents or traveling parent. Or, you could go look at photos of the family or pet. Or, maybe the child could make a list of all the things they loved the most about a dead pet. Better yet, if the child is up for it, bury the dead pet and ask family members to tell favorite stories about the pet.

There's not one strategy that will work for all kids. The key is to allow the child to experience the sadness and express it openly. That will help dissipate the sadness. Take the example of two-year-old Anna. Her dad regularly traveled out of town and Anna missed him greatly. Her mother struggled with getting Anna to bed because the sadness erupted at bedtime. Bedtime became a nightmare, dominated by "I miss my daddy" that she would wail through sobs.

At first, her mother tried to explain that Daddy had to travel for his job, that daddy would be home soon, and a variety of other tactics that were based in logic but failed to acknowledge the sadness. But when her mother said, "You really miss Daddy, don't you?" things began to improve. Well, sort of. Although the wailing got louder for a few minutes, the mother just let it occur and soon enough, it died down. Holding her mother tightly, the two-year-old resolved her own sadness. "He'll be home tomorrow." "Yes, sweetie, he will."

The child calmed down and was fast asleep in five minutes. What's remarkable about this story is that for months, the mother had been trying to reassure the child that Daddy would be home soon; yet, every bedtime was a cacophony of tears and protests. Only when the mother accepted her child's sadness did things improve.

Facing Their Fears

How should you handle a situation that frightens your child? Surprisingly, the answer is simple, at least for things you don't want the child to fear. Be gentle and with respect for the fear and a huge dose of reassurance, help your child face the fear. Children go through progressions in what they fear. A two-year-old is more likely to fear being separated from the parent, a five-year-old is more likely to fear "monsters" and "the dark," and a nine-year-old is more likely to fear real threats such as the death of a parent, being kidnapped, and so on.

✅ Fact

Anxiety is a generalized sense of worry or tension that does not have an identifiable cause or specific target. Fear, in contrast, is specifically focused on a person, animal, or thing, even imaginary things (e.g., dog, ghosts, etc.). Children can answer what's wrong with specificity if it's a fear.

The particular strategy you use to help a child overcome a fear depends on the age of the child and the source of the fear. Fear of being separated from a parent is real and palpable. Although your child may adapt well to some separations such as going to day care, other separations, such as being left with grandparents while the parents go on vacation, may be much harder to handle. The best antidote is preparation. Send along a family photo album, write notes that can be read to the child daily, participate in Skype phone calls, or whatever you can do to ease the tension.

For older children, help them conquer their (unreasonable) fears. It's good for children to be scared of some things (e.g., getting in a car with a stranger), so use your judgment. Take the case of seven-year-old Carrie. She had always loved playing in the ocean and her family gathered each summer for a big reunion at the beach. Suddenly, Carrie became scared to go in after she got a crab bite one day.

After discussion, Carrie's parents decided they did not want her to be afraid of the ocean. The whole family loved the beach and although a crab bite could hurt, it was no worse than a bee sting and the vast majority of parents still let their kids play outside. So, Carrie's parents developed a plan. First, the parents went in the ocean while she watched from the beach. Then, they stood hand in hand in very shallow water where crabs would be easy to spot as waves covered their feet. They took a couple of steps forward. Then, Carrie's dad picked her up and waded in a little deeper. Gradually, he lowered Carrie into the water, first letting her feet touch the water and then more gradually, letting more of her body touch the water while still holding her tightly. Then they took a break to build sand castles. After they got really hot, they repeated the above sequence, going a little farther each time. Within two days, Carrie was happily playing in the water again.

A Final Note: Emotions Are Healthy

Emotions are real and should be respected. Your child will be healthier, happier, and more successful in relationships if you embrace his emotions and teach him how to manage them. Being scared to acknowledge an emotion in yourself or others only serves to make the emotion more powerful in terms of the possible negative consequences. And, remember, expressing emotions does not mean that someone is emotional; in fact, the more someone expresses emotions verbally, the less his emotions churn inside of him only to burst out later in volcanic fashion.

CHAPTER 7

Independence

A llowing and encouraging children's independence may be one of the most difficult challenges of emotionally-intelligent parenting. After all, you don't want to overprotect your child, thwarting development and creating greater challenges for the child as she ages. But, you also want to avoid expecting too much independence too soon, setting your child up for failure and you for disappointment. What's the right balance? Surprisingly, for some issues, you can follow your child's lead because he will naturally express a desire for greater independence. Other than questions of safety, children typically give you accurate signals about what they are ready for; with safety issues, find ways to honor their independence while also keeping things safe.

What Is Independence?

Psychologist Erik Erikson wrote about children's desire for autonomy—a sense of purpose and self-determined activities—that begins in the toddler years. Independence is easy to recognize in two-year-olds whether it's the famous "no" or a more advanced "do it myself." Or, it may emerge in your child wanting to pick out her clothes and proudly wear mismatched colors and patterns that would challenge the ability of anyone to look at the outfit for too long without getting a headache. Or, you may find that she becomes much more opinionated about the need to take a nap or whether to put on a coat. What's a parent to do? In this chapter, you'll learn to think of this age as the "terrific twos" because learning independence is terrific!

Striving for independence takes on other forms, less frustrating ones for parents, as children progress through childhood. Any time they make an important decision (e.g., wanting to take a drama class) or engage in a challenging behavior (e.g., spending their first night away from home), and can do these things without undue need for emotional support, then they are exhibiting independence.

✅ Fact

Psychologist Erik Erikson wrote in 1950 about critical developmental tasks to accomplish at each age and stage of life. For toddlers, the key task to accomplish was *autonomy,* a synonym for independence. According to Erikson, if not allowed to develop autonomy, children would develop *doubt,* another way of saying they would experience a lack of confidence.

Why Learn Independence?

It's very important to recognize that developing autonomy or independence is a natural and *necessary* part of children's development. Does that mean you need to capitulate to every demand made by a two-year-old? No, but neither should you automatically say "no" or "do it because I said so," or systematically remove most choices from a toddler's life, or, for that matter, a pre-teen's life. So, even though your life may be easier if you tried to halt the independence train coming full force at you, you will compromise your child's healthy development. Specifically, you'll undermine your child's confidence in his ability to make a decision or take action without over-relying on emotional support or reassurance from others. Parents don't always make the connection between allowing their child to practice appropriate independence at various ages with the child's ability to function independently later in life. But, without practice, children will not gain the skill to be independent.

☺ Question

What if my child doesn't express a desire for independence and wants to rely on me for everything?
Pick some easy places to start encouraging independence such as picking out his own clothes, serving his plate, or completing an easy chore. And make sure you insist the child do it alone and then offer descriptions of what the child did and how well things turned out. Success being independent will lead to a desire for more independence.

If you support her independence—such as letting your two-year-old daughter pick out her own clothes and proudly wear the striped pants with a checked shirt, allowing your four-year-old to spend the night with a friend even though you have hesitations, or permitting your seven-year-old to play outside without your supervision—she'll be in a better position later in life to stand up to peer pressure, handle a change of schools, or attend university in another city. Your child cannot magically become independent if she hasn't been allowed to practice those skills earlier in life.

Supporting Independence at Different Ages

There are several challenges parents face when supporting independent development including getting over their own concerns or fears about the potential "risks" associated with the independence, coming to terms with the idea that it's okay for kids to make some decisions and that parents do not need to control everything, and letting a child be independent even when it may be annoying or inconvenient. Since the amount and type of independence varies by the child's age, it's important to think of independence as a series of developmental steps.

The next few sections will examine how to build independence at different age levels based on what's developmentally appropriate for children of that age. Developmentally appropriate doesn't mean that parents necessarily like what's going on—think about your teenage daughter out on a first date with an inexperienced teen driver—but that's important to the child's healthy growth in various areas of development. Sometimes parents resist allowing independence because it's anxiety provoking to allow the independence or because the child's efforts to be independent can sometimes look like misbehavior.

Independence at Two: The Terrific Twos

Yes, you read the title correctly. This age should be labeled "The Terrific Twos" rather than its oft-quoted alternative, "The Terrible Twos." What's terrible about a child wanting to become more self-determined and self-supporting? After all, your two-year-old is not asking to play alone in the yard or determine her bedtime. Instead, a two-year-old's attempts to become more independent are age-appropriate such as choosing what he wears, what he eats, or what books he has you read to him. Within limits, it's appropriate to let two-year-olds make as many decisions as possible as long as the results do not endanger their physical or emotional well being. Let's look at some of the common ways two-year-olds try to assert autonomy or independence.

Clothing Choices

You've planned a family picture and your two-year-old throws a fit about the outfit you chose. Or, it's the beginning of fall and you picked out long pants and your child wants to wear shorts. Or, the family is going out to dinner and you want your two-year-old to put on a nicer shirt, but the one he has on isn't dirty and it's his favorite shirt so he protests. Each of these situations is predictable as children begin to form a sense of self—including what the "self" likes or dislikes. What clothing to wear is a decision, and your two-year-old should *want to make this decision!* In other words, it's a good sign—developmentally, that is—that your child protests about the clothing you picked out for the family picture.

And, it would be so easy to avoid this kind of encounter that often leads to a power struggle between parents and kids over who is going to decide. Pick out two or three different things for the family picture that are all appropriate and let the child decide which one to wear. You've created a win-win situation with this simple choice; you are ensuring an "appropriate" outfit while your child still gets to make a decision. Maybe one of the outfits you picked out is scratchy, maybe one of them binds the child too tightly in the wrong place (some toddlers hate turtleneck shirts for this reason!), or maybe the colors aren't bright enough for your child. Put yourself in his place. Would you want someone making you wear a scratchy, binding, or dull outfit just because that person liked it?

Essential

Parents often display more caution with first-born children than second born and latter-born children. So, if you think you may be too cautious about "independence decisions," talk to a sibling or good friend who already has multiple children to get some perspective.

Some of you may be cringing a bit right now. After all, you're the adult. Shouldn't you be allowed to exert your authority and make the child wear the cutest or best outfit for the family picture? But, it's not a question of who is older (you are) or in charge (you are) or the responsible party (you are). Rather, it's a question of whether you're a confident enough parent who understands children's development. If so, you can allow your child to make simple decisions without believing that your authority has been threatened. Consider the following example.

Three-year-old Leah was set to go outside and play. Although it was January, the temperature that day was around 55°F. As Leah headed to the door her mother handed her a winter coat. Leah took the coat, threw it on the ground and said, "No, mommy, no." Instead of immediately reacting or possibly over-reacting to the inappropriate way her daughter was delivering the message, her mother calmly asked why she didn't want to wear that coat. Leah said, "Too hot." Knowing that her child did get hot easily, mom pointed to the coat rack and suggested that Leach pick out a coat. She picked a lighter-weight coat. At that point Leah's mom instructed her to pick up the other coat off the floor and hang it up. With a gentle voice she said, "I know you get hot easily. It's okay for you to pick out your coat. But, it's not okay to throw the coat down; just ask to wear a different one." Then they had a brief session during which Leah's mom helped her practice asking to wear a different coat instead of throwing it down.

But what about fashion faux pas? When Leah was two, her grandmother came to visit on a day when Leah chose a horribly mismatched outfit to wear. As Leah, her mother, and grandmother headed out to do some errands, the grandmother posed this question to her daughter, Leah's mom. "Are you going to let her go out looking like that? What will people think?" Leah's mom, confident of her decision to let Leah practice making minor "decisions" responded, "Well, I hope they'll think she has a mother who knows something about child development!" And, what if others don't think that? What if they judge you because of your child's clothing choices? The choice is clear—would you rather please those other people or support your child's healthy development? And, some of those "other people" would also approve of the mismatched outfit because they would realize the child picked out the clothes.

Food Fights

Babies have taste preferences and fullness cues from day one. They'll turn their head from a bottle of formula that tastes bad compared to mom's breast milk. And, they'll refuse to suck any more when their tummy is full, even though they've only eaten three ounces of the planned four ounces you thought they needed. So, why are you suddenly surprised when two-year-olds exercise the same preferences? Probably because they do it with such vehemence that it's easy to mistake a food preference for an issue of control.

When two-year-olds protest loudly or act out their frustrations, parents often join the battle and draw the proverbial line in the sand. Instead, step back and separate the issues. You can teach your young child the appropriate way to make a request known, such as Leah's mother did with her coat preference. Don't get locked into a battle though because of the *way* the child expressed her preferences.

So, if your two-year-old emphatically says "no" and dumps the plate full of peas on the floor, make the child help clean up the mess. Then give the child some guidance on a better way of expressing his opinion about peas. A simple "no" or "don't like peas" or just exercising a choice not to eat them—without dumping them on the floor—are all appropriate for that age. Then, and this is critical, do not force the child to eat the peas!

Again, some of you may question this advice. You may be wondering, "How can I back down when my child has behaved badly?" Remember, you did *not* back down from the inappropriate behavior of dumping the peas on the floor; instead, you made the child help clean up and also taught him a more appropriate way to refuse peas. The appropriate behavior, "no peas, Daddy" (or whatever you teach your child to do or say), needs to be recognized. Again, your child is expressing a reasonable preference and there are plenty of other healthy foods you can give him to eat.

But how will children expand their food palate if they don't try new things? First, their palate will naturally expand with age and exposure to different foods. And, as long as your child is well nourished and healthy, eating a wide variety of foods is not as critical to their overall development as is a healthy sense of independence.

ⓔ Alert

It's critical for spouses to agree about food, clothing, and other issues where children are apt to express independence. If one parent lets the child express food preferences and the other doesn't or even gets irritated, then the parents are sending a mixed-message to the child about the appropriateness of independence.

Here's one strategy that may work for you as you introduce new foods: Always offer the child at least two things you know he likes and that are healthy (turkey burger and apples; peanut butter sandwich and banana, chicken and green beans) and then introduce a third item with little or no fanfare. Children are curious and if the food looks appealing and smells good (to them!), they'll most likely try it. If they do and like the taste, they'll eat it. If they don't eat it, that's fine. Try something different tomorrow.

Food becomes a constant fight in some families. Yes, you can remove the option of dessert, not feed the child in between meals if they don't eat enough at the previous meal, and a whole host of strategies to coerce them to eat foods they don't like. But, you don't need to use coercion; take the battle for control out of it and let children make simple decisions. If your spouse fixes dinner and makes peas and you don't happen to like peas, you won't eat them. Or, most likely, your spouse will know you don't like peas and not force them on you. The parent-child food battles often have much less to do with nutrition than with your child's emerging awareness of his taste preferences and desire for independence. Allowing some choice takes away the battle and reinforces independence, a win-win solution.

The Proverbial "No" or "I'll Do It Myself"

If you've parented a two-year-old, sometimes it's easy to believe the only word they know is "no." Your child is learning autonomy and is exercising her right to have a different opinion from you. That's actually a healthy developmental sign. But how do you know when to force something on a child and when to allow her to exercise choice? Here's a simple rule to follow: If the issue involves safety or health, then there's no room to negotiate. A firm but kind response of, "It's not a choice" to your two-year-old who is fighting about getting in a car seat is the appropriate parental response. You can empathize ("I know you don't like to ride in the car seat") or even explain ("The car seat keeps you safe") and the wailing will likely continue. Stand firm. Safety issues are non-negotiable.

Deciding whether something is a safety issue can be more difficult than it sounds. Is it okay for your physically gifted two-year-old to climb to the top of the swing set and sit there? Or, to balance on a railing that's three feet off the ground? What about riding her three-wheeler down your driveway at speeds you consider too fast but delight her, and she stays in control and doesn't wreck? Safety issues exist at each stage of a child's life. Try to find win-win solutions; options that will encourage your child's independence and keep her safe. For the super-climber, provide climbing options that may be more appropriate than a swing set, "spot" the child, and perhaps even make her wear a helmet.

Finding win-win options applies to your child's growing desire to be more independent in other ways. Whether it's feeding, dressing, or walking instead of you carrying them, children often want to "do it myself." Yet, it can be an agonizing test of patience to walk at a two-year-old's pace or to wait the extra five minutes it seems to take to put on a pair of shoes and fasten the Velcro strap. What harm is there in doing things for them that they want to do for themselves?

You know the answer; give yourself a pep talk that goes something like this. "I'll be glad later when my child wants to do her homework without help, is able to wash her clothes, or can manage her money effectively. I'll be glad when my child trusts his judgment to make simple decisions rather than believing that his opinion doesn't matter. I'll be thrilled when my teenager leaves home at night to go out with friends and I don't have to fear her being sucked into dangerous situations because of peer pressure. I'll be glad that I encouraged my child to exercise independence and become confident in her ability to make decisions and take action without having to rely on others for approval." Give yourself that pep talk as often as needed when your child is two. The "terrific twos" may test your patience, but the outcomes are worth the effort.

When Two-Year-Olds May Crave Dependence

Parents also need to be mindful of opportunities to reinforce appropriate emotional independence. Whereas staying a weekend with grandparents may be easy for some two- or three-year-olds, it's a scary proposition for others. This type of emotional independence is critical to children's development and thus you need to be vigilant about creating opportunities. Your child should be able to trust multiple people to take care of him and not need just you. Your role is to help the child get comfortable with the new situation by describing what's going to happen, allowing your child to bring along comfort objects, and by easing the child slowly into new situations. What you don't want to do, however, is overly protect the child from situations that are perfectly safe.

Consider a child who is going from home care for the first two years of life to day care. If you choose a high-quality center with a good teacher-child ratio (1:4 is recommended with no fewer than one teacher per every six children), check references from other parents and make several visits with your child, then there comes a time when you must leave and not let your child cling to you as you fight to untangle her from your legs.

❓ Question

Should I allow my two- or three-year-old child to have a comfort object?
Absolutely! Comfort objects such as a favorite blanket or stuffed toy are just that. Children use them for emotional support to calm themselves when anxious or mad. Don't worry—your child will not want to take his teddy bear to first grade. As emotional skills build, children learn to self-comfort without the use of objects.

To help children face these times when they need to be apart from you, set up "goodbye routines." These routines can include special waves, honking the horn, reading a short book or any other rituals that the child can count on to help ease the transition from being in a parent's care to someone else's care.

Thus, your role as the parent of a two-year-old involves facilitating independence when the child may not want to be independent and allowing independence on issues where you may prefer to make choices for her. Think about it from the child's perspective. Going to a new day care to stay all day with adults the two-year-old child barely knows requires much more emotional strength and independence than picking out her clothes; yet, some parents worry about the child who cries at a new day care, but never think about giving the child reasonable choices related to food and clothes. Seems backward, doesn't it? Successful practice with independence equips children to be more independent.

Independence and Starting School

Beginning school brings a new set of challenges related to independence from riding a bus, to keeping up with your lunchbox, to remembering to give parents important messages or papers. Children who've successfully practiced being away from parents, making small decisions, and being responsible for some self-care will make this transition more easily.

Alert

Independence is just one facet of a successful school transition. But every child, regardless of academic skills, developmental level, or temperament can practice independence and be equipped to handle that part of the transition!

Come up with independence-building tasks your child is capable of doing—even though it may be challenging—and encourage the child's efforts to master the task. With each success, your child will more confidently pursue the next challenge with more independence. You may need to provide guidance or point out the consequences of some decisions (e.g., if you spend all of your allowance money the first day, then there's nothing left to spend later). Typically, your guidance and experience combine to form a powerful tandem to support children who are learning to be independent. Here are a few things that most five- to seven-year-old children should be able to handle independently.

- Chores such as feeding a dog, putting dirty clothes in a hamper, and picking up toys.
- Self-care tasks such as cutting their food, bathing, dressing, and putting their clean clothes in the drawer or in a closet (assuming they can reach the hangers!).
- Separations such as spending the night away from home with someone she knows well, going to a birthday party or sports practice without needing you to stay, and spending a week with grandparents while you and your partner travel.

- Decisions such as which sport to play, which activities to get involved in, how to spend a small allowance (sometimes the best teacher is making a mistake!), or who to invite to his birthday party.

Essential

Children's personalities differ, so obviously you need to calibrate your expectations of independence with your child's personality. For example, a shy child will be less comfortable the first day of kindergarten than an outgoing child and you should find ways to support that child's temperament while also promoting independence.

Independence Later in Childhood

As your child ages, the types of independent actions and decisions need to also change. For example, a ten-year-old is perfectly capable of doing his laundry, calling in the family pizza order on Friday night, or making a decision to participate in a year-round sport that requires lots of extra practice. This same ten-year old should typically be able to complete homework without a parent making sure he's on task or go to a week-long summer camp or with friends of the family on a beach vacation without the need to call home every day for reassurance.

Independence occurs in three major developmental areas: physical, financial, and social-emotional. Make sure you're providing opportunities to make decisions and practice independence in each area so that your child will be well balanced in all phases of independence.

CHAPTER 8

Assertiveness

Assertiveness is easy to confuse with independence, but they are two very different skills. Whereas independence addresses whether or not your child is comfortable working alone, making decisions appropriate to his age, and taking actions without an undue need for support, assertiveness involves taking up for yourself, protecting your rights, or stating your opinion. Assertiveness is more likely to be displayed verbally whereas independence is more likely to be displayed behaviorally. And sometimes they do occur together, such as Leah's declaration (assertiveness) that she wanted to wear a different coat (making her own clothing decision, which is independence).

What Is Assertiveness?

Some parents actively discourage the development of assertiveness in their children because they misunderstand the definition of it. Assertiveness involves:

- Declarative statements (I believe, I want, I think, I don't want that, I don't like that, and so on) that reveal his opinions, preferences, or needs
- Taking up for oneself or setting boundaries emotionally, socially, financially, or physically

- Respect for the other person
- Clarity of purpose that is aimed at standing up for oneself or sharing an opinion or belief

As such, assertive behavior does *not* involve any type of physical force, emotional pressure, or intimidation. Nor does it belittle or harm others in any way, and assertiveness is not used to manipulate other people. Although such behaviors can occur, they describe aggressiveness, not assertiveness.

 Fact

Males' average score on assertiveness is higher than females' average score. Be sure to set similar expectations for appropriate assertiveness for children of both sexes.

A Note about Passivity
Passiveness is the opposite of assertiveness. So, if you take the list above and reframe it to encompass the opposite behavior, you would be describing a passive person.

- No statements about personal wants or needs
- Not setting any boundaries with others; allowing others to take advantage of you, take you for granted, demand more than you want to give, or other similar actions
- Lack of self-respect (i.e., I'm not important enough for my needs or wants to matter to others)
- A lack of purpose or a tendency to conform, or follow others' lead without thought about whether that is a healthy and appropriate behavior; in other words, it's sometimes appropriate to follow others' lead, but not if you're doing so from a place of resignation, pressure, or lack of other options.

Why Should Children Learn Assertiveness?

There are a myriad of answers to the question about learning assertiveness, but a more simple way to examine this is to imagine situations your child may be in as she grows older. Do you want your teenage daughter to be able to say "no" to someone who is trying to take advantage of her? Do you want your teenage son to stand up to his peers when they talk about hazing an underclassman? Do you want your child to be able to easily join class discussions and feel comfortable stating an opinion? Do you want your child to be able to fend off potential bullies or stand up for another child who is being bullied? You're probably getting the idea that assertiveness is critical to healthy development and at times, to your child's safety. You cannot expect a child who has been trained to be passive to suddenly muster assertiveness. As the saying goes, "practice makes perfect."

Parenting Styles and Assertiveness

The child development field includes numerous studies related to different forms of parenting and the impact these can have on children. One commonly identified style is called "authoritarian" because of the emphasis the parent places on his authority and on the need for the child to passively follow what the parent expects or demands. Parents who subscribe to an authoritarian style are less likely to engage children in conversations about what went wrong and instead use some form of power-based discipline such as threats, spanking, yelling, or punishing harshly.

Parents who choose this style of parenting do not see the need for giving explanations to children and basically expect children to do something "because I said so." Unfortunately, this style of parenting can lead to timidity (passiveness) in children because speaking up is likely to lead to punishment. Not only are assertiveness skills unpracticed, but the modeling the child receives is more geared toward using power differences or threats to get what you want.

A contrasting style of parenting is the authoritative type. This style of parenting involves setting clear limits for children and explaining parental actions and rules to children so they can understand why they are being asked to do something. This style relies on reason-based forms of discipline including logical and natural consequences or a short time-out that is followed by what the child should have done differently. Warmth is high, threats are low, and children are encouraged to ask questions, make comments, or otherwise engage with parents. Contrary to what some might believe, authoritative parents have high standards and their children are usually well behaved because they understand the reason for or value of certain behaviors and because they want to do what the parent has requested, not out of fear of punishment but instead out of respect for the adult and an understanding of the request.

 Fact

There are other styles of parenting including a style that is commonly labeled "permissive" which involves high warmth but with few expectations and an "uninvolved" style where there is low warmth and low expectations. Children reared within these styles of parenting may be at greater risk of becoming aggressive because there are few parental boundaries or expectations for appropriate behavior.

Which Style Builds Assertiveness?

Which of the above parenting styles is more likely to yield a child who is assertive? The authoritative style. Why? Because the child has observed her parents explaining things to her (e.g., homework must be done before TV so that you're sure it's all completed thoroughly and when you are less tired), standing up for their rights in a calm way (e.g., no, you may not play tag inside the house), and using reason not anger or force to elicit others' cooperation (e.g., I need you to pick up your toys now so that I can vacuum the floor). But, even the most effective authoritative parents will have children who act out inappropriately at times. So, effective discipline styles are critical to effective parenting. The goal of discipline should be to teach. In fact, the word discipline comes from the Latin verb "discere" which means learn.

Remember Leah in Chapter 7 who threw her heavy coat on the floor? Expressing her opinion about which coat she wanted to wear was appropriate, but throwing the first coat on the floor was not. Leah's mom, an authoritative parent, made Leah pick up the coat (i.e., correct her mistake), but she also respected Leah's opinion about which coat would be most comfortable, reinforcing her daughter's assertiveness.

 **Essential**

> When children are assertive but also do something inappropriate at the same time, it's easy to discipline the wrong thing or discipline the assertiveness. Make sure to separate the child's willingness to state an opinion from any inappropriate actions such as yelling. Describe what the child did that was appropriate—stated an opinion—from the method of delivery.

But, what happens when a child of an authoritative parent disagrees with the parent? Doesn't the child take advantage of the authoritative parent's willingness to explain and engage in discussion? No, because authoritative parenting is also characterized by a willingness to set limits and have high expectations. Typically, the child will develop assertiveness but not aggressiveness, especially as she gets older and has more opportunities to practice assertiveness. And, sometimes, authoritative parents realize the child has a good point and may be influenced positively by the child's assertiveness.

Take the case of Carlos. His authoritative parents had set a rule that he must complete his homework before getting on his computer or watching TV. Carlos, a very high-energy fifth grader, came home from school with lots of pent-up energy. He found it difficult to sit down and do homework. He was constantly getting up or daydreaming, and getting his homework completed was becoming a point of contention between him and his parents. One day, Carlos asked his parents to have one hour of down time before he started his homework. He could play outside with friends, ride his bike, or anything else that would release energy. He proposed that computer or TV time still had to wait until after homework was completed. Carlos felt comfortable being assertive and his parents agreed with his plan. And, his attention to his homework improved.

What about the child of an authoritarian parent? How would he react to a situation such as the one Carlos faced? Typically, he would not speak up for fear of getting into trouble because he would be perceived to be challenging the parent's judgment. The passive behavior of not speaking up would mean the child continued struggling with concentration and produced a lower quality of work. But, what if the child of an authoritarian parent did speak up and question the homework-first rule? Often, the answer will be a repeat of the rule, "homework before computer or TV" with an accompanying line that basically reiterates that the parent is in charge and the kid should not question the parent. If the child persists, some type of power-based punishment is likely to follow. Have you heard the phrase "my way or the highway?" In a work place, the phrase is used to communicate that employees should either do what the boss wants or risk getting fired. Do employees ever have an idea that's better than the boss? Could children have an idea that's better than the parent's idea?

⚠️ Alert

Aggression involves an intent to harm the other person whereas assertiveness does not! Aggression will involve physical, emotional, or social harm to the recipient and it will be clear the aggressive party wanted those outcomes.

Let's go back to Carlos for a minute. His solution would be considered assertive because he stated a belief (I'll do better on homework if I don't have to start it right away) and took care of himself (a physical need to blow off some energy and an academic need to be able to concentrate better). So, in this case, Carlos's solution was a compromise with his parents. Both he and his parents were assertive—him to request an hour to blow off energy and them to insist that homework be completed before TV or computer time—allowing Carlos to see the benefits of speaking up and taking care of himself and also the benefits of standing your ground, as his parents did when they insisted that homework must be completed before computer or TV time begins. A win-win solution was fueled by assertiveness.

Simply put, you cannot expect children to be assertive with other people or in other situations if you don't encourage them to practice that skill. Moreover, if you're communicating that assertiveness is bad or wrong, you're also making it much more difficult for them to want to gain this skill because they are likely to view it as "wrong" or "offensive" or "aggressive."

Examine Your Attitudes about Assertiveness

Before you can teach a child assertiveness, you must first be willing to allow it and even recognize its benefits. If you are the type of parent who is uncomfortable giving children choices, providing explanations, or letting children disagree with you, then teaching assertiveness will be like trying to walk in quicksand. You won't get anywhere. You must convince yourself that the value to your child of being assertive outweighs the need to command instant obedience or have to explain a decision. Explaining one of your decisions or rules—such as why a pre-teen has to clean her room when it's her space—does not undermine your authority as a parent. If your boss explains a decision she made to you, do you respect her more or less? Are you more likely to work effectively with a boss who explains herself or one who just says, "Do it" and doesn't provide reasoning? Although you are likely to comply, your work satisfaction will probably be lower.

What about Respect for Authority Figures?

Some of you may be thinking, "It's fine for my child to be assertive with other kids, but not with adults because that's disrespectful." Given that appropriate assertiveness is never rude, confrontational, angry, or blaming, then how can it be disrespectful? Is it disrespectful to stand up for yourself, to offer an opinion, or ask for an explanation? If you answered any of those situations with a "yes," then you're giving your child a double message—it's okay to be assertive (disrespectful in your mind) with peers but not with authority figures.

Children have a keen radar for inconsistencies, especially those that cannot be easily justified. Remember, assertiveness is not rudeness and involves no intent to harm the other person; so, why is it okay to be assertive with a peer but not an authority figure? And, given that some "peers" can be authority figures—the senior captain of the soccer team, for example—the line becomes even more blurry. Most likely, the problems with hazing, bullying, and other forms of dominating or cruel behavior will not stop until the targets or victims—and the bystanders who watch without directly participating—have enough assertiveness skills to stop it.

Think about the Possible Consequences

If you're not comfortable letting children be assertive with authority figures, there are two things to consider. First, imagine a future situation in which your child needs to stand up to an authority figure to protect himself. Your child, if feeling nauseous and faint, will need to stand up to a coach that instructs kids to run laps in oppressive heat. Would you rather your child stand up to the coach or suffer from heat exhaustion? Your son or daughter, unfortunately, may need to say "no" with conviction to inappropriate behaviors by a very small minority of misguided adults. While these occurrences, thankfully, are rare, a child needs to be assertive enough to tell someone else what happened. Perpetrators aren't likely to pick targets that possess assertiveness skills. If you have taught your children never to question an authority figure, they will find it hard to muster the necessary assertiveness when the time comes.

 Fact

About 20 percent of all child abuse is perpetrated by someone other than a parent, with the largest subgroup being other relatives, who account for 7 percent. That leaves 13 percent of all cases of child abuse that are perpetrated by someone else, typically someone the child knows such as a teacher, coach, camp counselor, and so on.

A second consideration is that because assertiveness is a skill, a lack of practice with assertiveness when young will leave your child ill-prepared to be assertive with peers when the peer asks to copy your child's completed homework, tries to convince your child to engage in inappropriate behavior (e.g., drinking, smoking, drugs, etc.), or begins bullying your child or one of her friends. Almost every parent would agree that these situations call for a child to be skillful at standing her ground or confronting someone else. That takes practice. And, it takes clear communication and support from the parents that assertiveness is not only okay, but also necessary and expected in those situations.

Teaching Assertiveness

There are three primary ways you can teach a child to be assertive. First, you must identify when to be assertive. Second, you must model assertiveness yourself. Third, actively teach the techniques of assertiveness to your child and support her efforts at assertiveness.

Identify When to Be Assertive

If you are able to tune into your own emotions, they will cue you about when assertiveness is appropriate and necessary. For example, if you are confused or want clarification, assertiveness in the form of asking a question is appropriate. If you're irritated or angry, identify whether another person contributed to those emotions and if so, be assertive by using an "I" message (see Chapter 6). "I" messages also work if you're feeling anxious or scared that someone else might be upset, such as one mom felt about calling a doctor on call at home over a holiday weekend. If she had initiated the call with, "I'm very worried because my son's pain level has increased substantially," almost no doctor in the world would be annoyed at that opening statement. In fact, most would respect the fact that you called and did not let the situation worsen.

If you're feeling frustrated because someone is taking advantage of you, making you do things you believe are inappropriate or unnecessary, assertiveness in the form of "No, I won't do that because..." is very appropriate. Or, you could use an "I" message again, such as "I'm uncomfortable doing _____ and would like to discuss that with you." Your feelings will be a clear guide about situations that call for assertiveness. Pay attention to those feelings and have verbal responses or behaviors ready to employ to help you be more assertive, especially when the stakes are high.

⚡ Essential

High-stakes situations such as not getting in a car with a stranger, not opening the front door when home alone, and other situations that call for assertiveness must be discussed and even practiced with your child. Make the practice serious but not scary.

Model Assertiveness

Assertiveness skills don't just materialize in situations when they would be valuable or even necessary. Rather, well-meaning and very loving parents who don't model assertiveness may be inadvertently teaching children the opposite of assertiveness. Take the case of Jerome's mom. One Friday afternoon, she took Jerome to the doctor because of severe nausea and pain. The doctor did a quick exam, asked some questions, and concluded that it was probably food poisoning or a virus and that Jerome should go home. When Jerome's mom asked if it was typical to be in this much pain with food poisoning, the doctor gave a vague answer and assured them by tomorrow he would be better. Later that night, though, Jerome got worse. Jerome's mom didn't want to call the doctor and disturb him at home and she had already asked the pain question once, so what would she ask about? So they waited until the morning. By then, Jerome's pain was excruciating and his mom got scared and took him immediately to the hospital. He had a kidney stone. If his mother had been more assertive the day before in the office or in her willingness to call the doctor during off hours, maybe Jerome would have been treated sooner. But, if you're taught not to ask questions of authority figures, it's hard to learn that skill even as an adult.

Children will watch your interactions with others and learn from those as much as they do from what you teach them directly. They will learn these skills if they see you modeling assertiveness;

unfortunately, they can also learn to be aggressive or passive by watching you.

 **Question**

> **How can you be sure that assertiveness won't backfire and result in the other person refusing to help you, becoming aggressive, or having some other response that may harm you?**
> Anyone who responds to assertiveness with aggression or other inappropriate behaviors would probably act that way regardless of whether you were assertive or not. Passivity may seem to keep things calm in the moment, but it rarely works in the long run. The abused child who avoids the abusive parent still gets abused. Assertiveness is more likely to prevent mistreatment by others than any other behavior.

Assertiveness Techniques

Children who are able to recognize their feelings have mastered the first step in assertiveness, but there's more to learn. Paying attention to their feelings will help children identify situations that may call for assertiveness. For example, your child may be frustrated that soccer practice got called off due to rain, but that doesn't call for assertiveness. Frustration fueled by another kid trying to copy her homework does call for assertiveness. Sadness caused by being made fun of calls for assertiveness. Anger caused by being embarrassed by an older sibling in front of friends calls for assertiveness. Help your child identify feelings and then let those feelings and what triggered them be the guide for the next step.

Assertive Statements

As children are sharing the events of the day with you, pay attention to opportunities for assertiveness and discuss those with the child. "What did you do when Rose tried to copy your math homework on the bus ride to school?" If your daughter refused to let Rose copy her work, praise her for setting a boundary. If your daughter gave in (she didn't want to share her homework but didn't know how to say "no"), then you need to teach her "I" messages. Teach her to say something like "I'm uncomfortable giving you my homework because the teacher said to do it by ourselves." Or, a simple "No, I'm not willing to share my homework" may be all that's called for. Use phrases like "setting boundaries" or "saying no" or "giving your opinion" or "standing up for yourself" to help children connect their emotions to assertive words and behaviors.

Assertive Actions

As your child gets older, there will be more and more opportunities for assertive actions, not just words. The pre-teen who stands between a bully and a friend who is being bullied is demonstrating assertiveness. Or, the child who walks away from a situation he doesn't want to be involved in or shouldn't be involved in is demonstrating assertiveness. The child who is willing to go ask for a teacher's help when he is feeling overwhelmed about something is demonstrating assertiveness. A younger child who can stand up to an older sibling—one who is being paid to babysit but is ignoring the younger child while texting friends for hours—deserves recognition and support from the parents.

Question

What assertive actions should a child take with a bully?
Teach your child to make eye contact, and in a firm and strong voice say something like "I won't let you bully me." Then, the child needs to continue confident and assertive behaviors such as sitting where he wants to, not giving away his lunch money, or telling the child to "stop it" if the bully acts out again. Your child should also seek adult help.

Assertiveness not only protects your child from bullying, unwanted actions, or unfair manipulation by others, it also gives her something very positive—a belief that she's important enough that, even when the stakes are lower, she can ask for an explanation, state her opinion, or say no to an unreasonable or untimely request. Assertiveness reinforces one's sense of self and self-value. Your willingness to embrace assertiveness in your children may be enhanced if you frame assertiveness as demonstrating self-respect rather than disrespect to others.

CHAPTER 9

Interpersonal Relationships

Interpersonal relationships may be the emotional intelligence skill that comes most naturally to children. Any time they are playing with a friend, cuddling with a parent, or helping a preschool teacher take care of the classroom gerbil, they are developing interpersonal relationship skills. Even though these behaviors come naturally to most children, there are skills to be learned that will help children seek and purposefully develop relationships later in life.

What Do Interpersonal Relationships Involve?

Adult relationships can be an enigma—open and communicative or closed and quiet, full of trust or mistrust, characterized by mutuality or by self-interest, validating or confidence shaking, nurturing or distant—all these outcomes rely heavily on the *skills* developed earlier in life. What your children see you do, how you interact with them, what they observe between you and your partner, what messages you teach them about the value of relationships, and the skills you actively teach about communication will affect their attitudes and skills related to forming meaningful and mutual relationships with others.

Possessing good skills in interpersonal relationships means your child knows how to connect with others she barely knows, build a relationship, and develop mutuality, trust, and vulnerability in her closest relationships.

Interpersonal Relationships Are Important for Children

It's easy to understand why relationships are important to adult success. Whether it's forging a loving romantic relationship, building an effective team at work, working through a challenge with a neighbor, or getting a first job, relationship skills are critical to success. Some children master the art of relationships early in life. Perhaps they are spurred on by a genetic tendency to be more outgoing or the skills they've copied from parents. For others, especially those who are genetically shy, who don't have a chance to observe healthy relationships, or are not taught effective relationship skills, the challenge is much greater.

Question

What about shy children or those who just happily play alone—should they be made to interact?
Yes. Relationships are vital for our emotional well-being and the skills to be successful in relationships are not intuitive to all children, and perhaps especially difficult to learn for shyer children. That's even more reason to give them plenty of practice. But, the practice opportunities you provide should consider and be respectful of their temperament. In other words, don't send a shy child to summer camp for a week at age eight and expect them to be cured of the shyness.

By middle school, your child's peer relationships will become a central part of his life. Middle school can be a brutal experience for those who are lacking skills the peer group values—whether it's being able to excel in sports or talk about the latest song releases by a favored artist. Understanding how relationships work and demonstrating skill in them will be a vital part of your child's life from middle school through adulthood.

Key Elements of Successful Relationships

Think about your most successful relationships. What characterizes them? More than likely, your answer involves most of the following: trust, respect, mutual give and take, the ability to be yourself and be accepted for who you are, shared activities you both enjoy, emotional intimacy or being able to share information that makes you feel vulnerable, caring about the other person, and the ability to resolve conflict effectively.

Successful relationships are not accidental. Thriving in relationships requires skills. Here's a list of skills you can help children learn that will increase their effectiveness with others.

- How to start a conversation with someone he doesn't know
- How and when to move a conversation from a surface level to a more meaningful level
- How to compromise
- How to resolve conflict
- How to give and take
- How to build trust
- How to make an emotional bid—or an attempt to connect with the other person
- How to make the relationship fun

Children's Friendships: Experiencing and Practicing Relationships

Children's friendships give them a chance to practice effective relationship skills as well as the ups and downs of relationships. These relationships are far more important than most adults probably recognize in terms of their value to children learning how to initiate, develop, and maintain relationships skills.

Who Is That Other Baby?

Even as a young infant, babies will attune to another baby or young child more than they will an adult. First cousins Zachary and Katie were born the same week. At six month of age, both now able to sit up, they were put on a blanket facing each other in a sitting position. Katie reached out her hand and patted Zach's face. He squealed and returned the favor. They took turns touching and laughing until Katie reached out a little too hard and sent Zach teetering backward. Unfazed and unhurt, Zach sat back up and the game continued. Yes, it was a game. What do infants learn from these interactions? They learn that other people, particularly ones who seem to be a lot like them (size, features, etc.) can be lots of *fun*. They experience joy. They learn the beginning of mutual interaction (think about Katie and Zach touching each other's faces). They learn when to forgive and move on such as Zach's willingness to keep playing after Katie caused him to tumble backward.

 Fact

> Infants are so attuned to each other that typically, if one infant begins to cry—say in a day care setting or hospital newborn nursery—many others will follow suit. And, they can tell the difference between a tape recording of their own cry and that of a different infant's cry. Infants are born ready to socialize.

Toddler and Preschool Friendships

Katie, at twenty months, had a fourteen-month-old friend named Anna. Actually, Katie and Anna did not pick each other as friends. Instead, they often played together because their parents were good friends with each other. But because of their familiarity with each other, whenever they were together, they played easily with each other, even though each had an older sibling.

Anna had a kitchen play set and she and Katie would take turns "cooking" when the families gathered at Anna's house. Anna and Katie would initiate interactions with each other by holding up something for the other to see. They would laugh or smile at each other. They would offer to feed their parents and giggle with joy at parents eating the make-believe food. The toddlers played happily side by side, not needing words to cement their friendship. Their familiarity and comfort with each other allowed for sharing the space without controversy.

And what did they learn about relationships? First, they learned how to share the same space and share the toys. Though occasional disputes arose related to sharing a cooking utensil, they quickly forgot their anger or frustration as soon as the dispute was resolved. In essence, they learned to "forgive and forget." They also had the lessons of infancy reinforced—relationships can make things more fun and bring joy to life. Playing with a friend is something to anticipate.

Preschool children engage in even more sophisticated interactions. They now do more "choosing" of their own friends based on their enjoyment of similar toys or activities. And, they're more likely to play cooperatively, such as building a tower together or playing games. And, they're more likely to experience conflict precisely because they are engaging more cooperatively with peers. Scarce toys or two preschoolers who both want to be the "teacher" while others pretend to be "students" will create conflict. And, children at this age begin to anticipate seeing their good friends and associate friendship with fun.

What can you do as a parent to build the foundation for future relationships? First, reinforce the lessons of sharing. Because toddlers and preschool children cannot take someone else's emotional perspective, sharing can be difficult. Even though they probably won't understand why, make them share and explain why by saying things such as, "both of you want to play with that toy, so you need to take turns; I'll set a timer and when it rings, give the toy to Anna." (Actually it's best to use an old-fashioned hourglass timer with sand so that children can see how much time is left before the toy gets shared.) Sharing is the first lesson in give and take and mutuality is critical to successful relationships. Sharing also creates trust—each child is assured that the other is willing to give up the valued toy.

🄴🄾 Alert

An important skill in relationships is to admit your mistakes. So, begin teaching children during their toddler and preschool years to say, "I'm sorry" or "I was wrong." But, don't expect them to say it with much empathy for the other person. Remember, kids at this age have trouble taking other's emotional perspectives. That should not give them a free pass to never admit a mistake though.

Another thing you can do is teach children how to resolve conflict. If conflict does erupt, bring the children together, have each one tell you what happened, and then help them try to see the others' perspective (again, this will be difficult for them to fully grasp, but that's okay). Then, get them to suggest possible solutions, and work with them (perhaps giving them some ideas) until they come up with a solution they both can accept. This is called compromise and it's a skill your child will need!

Another thing you can do is to ensure that your child has ample opportunity to play with other children. Even if one parent chooses to stay at home with the children, make sure a toddler or preschooler interacts with age-mates several times a week. It's critical for preschool children to practice sharing, recovering from minor disputes and returning to happy play, and experiencing the fun of relationships. They also need practice being comfortable around other children they don't know and learning how to reach out and invite someone to play or enter the play of an existing group. And, they need to practice basic relationships skills such as assertiveness (e.g., "I want to play with that toy") and emotional expression when someone else grabs a toy without asking (e.g., "I'm mad").

Friendships and Proximity

Now five years of age, Katie has started kindergarten. At school, she is most likely to play with the other girls (yes, there's an early gender bias with playmate selection), particularly those who sit at her table, ride her bus, or play on the same soccer team. Friendship, at this age, is largely influenced by convenience (who's available or nearby), shared activities (soccer, Girl Scouts), or a shared interest in a specific toy or game. Thus, a child may have several friends, the one that lives next door, the one she hangs out with the most at soccer practice and asks to have spend the night, or the new friend from school. Friendships at this age do not have much loyalty though, as evident when children say things like "I'll be your best friend if you . . . " (e.g., give me your candy, share that toy). And most parents have heard the familiar refrain when a child gets upset, "I'm not your friend anymore."

 **Question**

> **Why do school-age children seem to prefer playing with members of the same sex?**
>
> Because of the way we socialize boys and girls—dressing them differently, introducing different sports, engaging them in different types of play with parents, offering them different toys, and even allowing more assertiveness and aggression in boys—kids tend to like playing better with members of their own sex because that child is most likely to have the same interests and style of play. Having said that, many male-female friendship pairs find plenty of common play interests and parents should encourage such.

What does your child learn about relationships at this stage? Katie now understands the concept of "friend" as someone whom you choose to interact with more than other people. This age brings more opportunities to get feelings hurt, feel left out, or feel awkward if you're the child standing on the outside of a group looking in. In other words, children begin to learn that while relationships can bring much joy, they can also bring sadness.

How can you promote their relationship skills at this age? This is the age to teach children, if you've not already done so, how to reach out effectively to others to begin a relationship. Teach them what to say to a child who's new in the class, how to join a group already at play, or how to ask someone to play with them. With shy children, use stuffed animals or other family members to help you role play interactions with other kids. Help children develop sentences they can use such as, "I like to . . . Want to do that with me?" The child who wants to join a group needs to learn strategies that will work such as, "Can I play too?" or "This looks like fun" while going to the back of the line of kids that are happily running through a sprinkler set up in a neighbor's yard. Shy children in particular don't know what to say or how to join and sometimes watch glumly from a distance or a window. Or, they hang around the edges, hoping someone will invite them to join, not realizing it's okay to invite yourself to join. Or, they make awkward overtures like pulling the hose, which moves the sprinkler closer to them, angering other kids in the process.

Elementary School Children and Friendships

By age eight or nine, children's friendships become more complex. Children understand much better why they like one person better than another and what they enjoy about spending time together. So, even though Katie may be in a different class than her best friend from last year, she's likely to stay connected to this friend from a year ago if they have common interests and "click" with each other. There's also a sense of loyalty. Descriptions about why this person is a friend tend to center more on characteristics of the person such as, "She's really funny" rather than, "We're on the same soccer team." And, an important addition at this stage, children begin to understand the concept of trust and mutuality. They expect their friends to be nice to them and understand that they are expected to be nice as well.

What do children learn about relationships at this stage? First, they begin to understand better that friendships involve more than just doing things together. They appreciate the other person's qualities and how those qualities (e.g., a sense of humor, creativity) affect them. They can, unfortunately, learn about violation of trust or lack of mutuality and how much that can sting. But, these incidents, if they occur, also give your child the opportunity to learn how to repair trust and overcome disappointment.

What can parents do to promote interpersonal relationship skills at this age? First, help children understand what trust means and how that applies to relationships. For example, if your child has accepted an invitation to spend a Friday night with a friend and then later learns that her soccer team is going out for pizza after their 6 P.M. game, she has an important decision to make. Does she cancel the overnight, not go out with her team, or try to do both and arrive at her friend's house after 8:30 P.M. instead of around 7 P.M.? Talk to her about commitments, trust, and what she would want if the situation were reversed. Sometimes you need to make choices that bolster an important relationship—going to her friend's house right after the game—in order to demonstrate the value you put on the relationship. And, if the situation were reversed, your daughter would probably expect or at least hope that her friend would make the same choice. That's where mutuality and loyalty come in.

You can also strengthen the skills she may need to reach out to new friends. Each year there will be new kids on the soccer team, in the classroom, or at the Girl Scout meeting. Teaching your child the building blocks of conversation (see the section later in this chapter) will help her reach out effectively to kids she wants to become friends with.

🔴 Alert

It can be devastating to see your child not invited to birthday parties or not able to integrate herself with age-mates in social situations. Seek feedback from teachers and others who have the opportunity to observe your child interact with others. There could be many reasons for the lack of friendships—including shyness, being different in some way, having poor interaction skills, or even depression. Try to understand the root issues and deal with those first.

Pre-Teen and Teen Friendships

By the pre-teen years (eleven or twelve), children focus even more heavily on trust and loyalty, and add emotional intimacy to the list of characteristics that define a friend. Katie, at this age, looks to friends as people she can talk to when upset, share a secret with, or rely on to help her deal with a problem. Especially during middle adolescence (fourteen or fifteen) friends become the center of a child's life, replacing the parents as the "go to person" when a problem arises. Adolescent friendships are intense but ripe with betrayal and other harsh lessons. Rifts in a friendship, whether created by a perceived slight or outright betrayal, exact a critical toll on children's trust, especially if the relationship is not repaired or the misunderstandings are never addressed.

Lessons your child learns at this age involve how to garner someone else's trust, reach compromises, be vulnerable (emotional intimacy), and repair relationships when things go wrong.

What can you do as a parent to support learning of interpersonal relationship skills in teens? Because many teens and preteens don't talk with their parents a lot about their friendships, especially problems in their friendships, your most powerful tool is modeling the values and skills you want your child to adopt. So, let your child see you maintaining your own close friendships outside the family circle, share examples of how you and a friend worked out a disagreement, discuss friendship dilemmas and choices you had to make, and what values (trust, loyalty, etc.) you were relying on to help you make the best decisions when you experienced trouble in relationships.

 Question

What should I do if my child is in a clique?
In academic terms, cliques are small groups of early teens, usually all the same-sex, who hang out together and are all friends. Being a member of a clique predicts academic and social competence for girls but not boys. So, cliques are not necessarily bad. Being intolerant of those who are different or bullying others is what needs to be stopped, so make sure you talk to your child about acceptance of differences and respect for all people.

Basic Skills to Build Interpersonal Relationships

If your child can master the following four skills, he'll be well on his way to developing a strong foundation of interpersonal skills: reading cues in a social environment, mastering the levels of a conversation, responding to emotional bids, and dealing with conflict.

Effective Reality Testing

Effective reality testing, a skill you will learn more about in Chapter 12, will enable your child to scan the environment for clues about when it's appropriate to approach an individual or group. For example, if another child is busily playing with just one other child and together they have built a large tower, this isn't a good time for your child to insert himself in the group. On the contrary, if two kids have just emptied a basket of blocks on the floor, this is a much better time to enter the play.

Teach your child to be aware of other cues such as the amount of materials available. For example, three kids sharing one basketball may be the maximum unless your child suggests playing a game of two on two. Also, teach him to pay attention to cues from others that may be nonverbal invitations (waving to your child, looking in his direction and smiling) to join the group at play. These insights may sound overly sophisticated for younger children, so adjust your language and how much you point out. Even a four-year-old can understand that if there are four children and three tricycles, someone isn't going to be part of that group. Knowing how to suggest sharing or how to find another group that is "open" will spare your child lots of potential frustration and possible blows to his self-regard.

Mastering the Levels of Conversation

Have you ever been interacting with another adult and she made you uncomfortable because she shared emotionally intimate information too soon in your relationship? For example, suppose you offer to take a new colleague in your department out to lunch during her first week of employment. Over lunch she shares the heartbreak of a recent broken engagement and how depressed she's been for four months. She also shared that she's entered therapy to help herself get straightened out. This level of emotionally intimate sharing would make most people very uncomfortable upon first meeting someone, and thus they would retreat, making a lasting relationship even more unlikely. At the other end of this spectrum is the adult who can never get beyond the facts—the events of the day, the new article of clothing, or his plans for an upcoming vacation. You may spend lots of time with this person without ever knowing him well.

In general, your child's conversations should progress from facts and data (who your teacher is, whether you play soccer) when first meeting a friend to a more interesting level if a friendship is going to develop. The next level of emotional intimacy is sharing aspects of who you are (e.g., how much you like soccer, what you think of some computer game) that are age appropriate. Next, the sharing becomes a little more intimate such as sharing joys or frustrations (e.g., your child shares that he's bummed the coach doesn't start him, or his excitement about scoring the most goals in a game). Finally, there's a level of emotional intimacy saved for only your closest friends and that most children won't be capable of until the pre-teen or teen years. A teen telling his best friend that he hates soccer but is scared to quit because he thinks it will disappoint (or anger) his parents requires a deeper level of trust and connection with the other person.

 **Essential**

Avoid discriminating against your son when teaching emotional intimacy. He'll need that ability to form loving and healthy relationships as an adult. So, don't think of emotional intimacy as something only females should have or that the female in a relationship will be responsible for ensuring it. Relationships require two people, both willing to connect with others.

Another helpful tool in learning how to start and sustain conversations involves the use of questions. While a closed-ended question, one that can be answered with a simple yes or no, is sometimes appropriate (e.g., Can I join your game?), more meaningful conversations are built around open-ended questions. So, a teen who is trying to get to know a new girl who just moved to town might ask, "What sports do you like to play?" That question opens the possibility for richer conversation, even if the other person responds that she doesn't like sports!

Responding to Emotional Bids

Psychologists use the term "emotional bids" to refer to attempts to connect with others, whether it's on a surface level or a more emotional level. The previous section covered ways that your child can initiate emotional bids. Responding to emotional bids from others is just as important. In essence there are three ways to react when someone else attempts to connect with your child—your child can "accept" the invitation and engage with the other child, your child can ignore the invitation and the other child, or your child could respond in an inappropriate or aggressive way. Only one of those responses builds healthy and long-lasting relationships. So, it's important to teach your child—both directly and by modeling—that when someone else makes a bid for his attention, he should respond appropriately. Parents, often caught in the rush of working a full-time job and managing a household, sometimes inadvertently ignore or respond inappropriately to bids from their children. Let's say a five-year-old approaches a parent working on a huge and thankless project such as cleaning out an over-stuffed garage. "Will you play a game with me?" can be responded to by mumbling something and continuing to work (thus ignoring the child), by showing frustration ("can't you see I'm really busy now") or by responding appropriately. Appropriate responses would include everything from taking a fifteen-minute break to play, to inviting the child to help with the garage clean-up, to smiling and letting the child know when you will be free to play. Children who get ignored or rebuffed learn not to make emotional bids and they also learn it's okay to ignore or rebuff others who try to connect with them.

Dealing with Conflict

There are entire books written about how to manage conflict, so it's clearly an important relationship management skill. Other emotional intelligence skills learned in this book, if applied in conflict situations, will help your child effectively manage conflict.

Emotional self-awareness enables your child to understand what is making him angry and *emotional expression* allows him to express it appropriately to the right people, alerting them that something is wrong and he needs their help to fix it. *Assertiveness* ensures your child will not be taken advantage of by others and gives him the ability to bring up difficult topics. The trust, loyalty, and mutuality that result from effective *interpersonal relationship skills* provide a better foundation from which to discuss sensitive issues and to reach decisions that allow the relationship to continue. *Empathy* will enable your child to understand the other child's perspective, a necessity in conflict resolution. *Problem solving* and *impulse control* will give your child skills for thinking about possible solutions to a problem (conflict), and control over impulses will ensure that your child does not lash out or lose patience during the conflict. That list of skills may sound overwhelming; but, the sooner your child begins learning and practicing each of these, the more likely he will be to resolve conflict effectively. Interpersonal relationships that do not have some conflict tend to be stuck at a very surface level and thus, do not provide great meaning or joy.

 **Essential**

Teach your child to look for win-win solutions to all conflict rather than win-lose or even a compromise that may result in both parties feeling like things were resolved in a lose-lose way. In other words, teach your child to look for solutions that meet both people's needs.

Interpersonal Relationships and the Shy Child

Psychologist Jerome Kagan has studied shy children for decades. First, it's important for parents to understand that shyness is a temperament characteristic children are born with, just as they are born with different activity levels. When a shy child is put into a new situation and with new people, her body is flooded by a strong physiological reaction, the same reaction you experience when facing lots of stress. In other words, new people and new situations are very stressful for shy children. This physiological flooding that occurs makes it harder for her to think clearly and naturally urges her to seek the type of environment that will stop the unpleasant physiological flood. Hence, she may cling to your leg, refuse to go inside, cry or engage in any number of other behaviors. Parenting a shy child takes lots of patience and a willingness to help them practice interpersonal skills.

Alert

Shyness can be embarrassing to parents. When all the other five-year-olds run onto the field for the first soccer practice and yours clings to you on the sideline, it can be very uncomfortable. If you're a parent who tends to feel uncomfortable, let your own feelings of discomfort give you empathy for your child. Whatever discomfort you're feeling is probably much stronger in your child who is facing this new situation. Be patient and calm as you help the child get comfortable. Anger, irritation, or threats will not make the shyness disappear.

When the shy child enters a new day care, he may find it difficult to join groups. Enlist the teacher's help to "coach" your child through situations. For example, if your child is standing off to the side watching a group play a game, the teacher could go up and ask your son if he wants to play. If he does, the teacher should help him understand what actions would be appropriate. Sometimes just joining the group with an "I'm playing now" is fine—such as when kids are playing tag. Sometimes the child needs to let others know he wants to play "I want to play too." Picking the right time to say this can make the difference between a warm welcome and not being heard.

As your shy child grows, you may have to set up opportunities to learn skills. For example, if he wants to go to the latest Avenger movie, require him to invite a friend to go along to the movie and out for an ice cream cone later. Shy kids do better in one-on-one situations, so set them up for success. As he gets even older, teach him skills for all different types of conversations. For example, ten-year-old Charlie was very shy and had been since birth. Every Friday night his family ordered pizza and shared it while watching a movie together. One Friday night Charlie asked whether the pizza had been ordered. It hadn't, and so his mom gave him the phone number asked Charlie to call in the order. He froze. Thirty minutes later after lots of coaching about what to say and what the person taking the order would probably ask, Charlie finally mustered the courage to place the call. Such it is for shy kids. The interpersonal skills that come so easily to other children can be painfully slow and difficult to develop. It's your responsibility as an adult to work with the child to improve his skills, thus lessening the anxiety.

CHAPTER 10

Empathy

E mpathy. Some adults hear that word and immediately conjure up images of being taken advantage of or having to agree with someone. Not true! Empathy requires neither submission nor agreement. The only things it does require are a willingness to listen and to understand the other person's perspective. Sounds easy, but it's not; empathy may be the single most challenging emotional intelligence skill to learn, partially because it requires attending to others more in a given moment than attending to oneself.

What Does Empathy Involve?

Empathy first requires someone to *be able to take the other person's perspective*; in other words, the basis of empathy is a *cognitive* skill. Preschool children have a very limited ability to take someone else's perspective. Think about your two-year-old playing hide and seek. As you began counting, she ran to a different part of the same room you were in and stood facing the wall with her hands covering her eyes. She thought she was well hidden! She was unable to cognitively imagine what you could see or she would have chosen a much better hiding place.

Preschoolers find it even more challenging to imagine someone's emotional perspective—that's way more abstract than where someone is sitting or standing—and thus, they say things that can hurt others' feelings. Five-year-old Robby answered the phone one day and he recognized the voice on the other end. So, he called his mother to the phone by saying, "Mom, it's that lady that talks so long. She wants to talk to you." Robby got in big trouble for what he considered just being honest. But, his age made it unlikely that he would be able to put himself in the caller's place and imagine her embarrassment. Or, take the case of four-year-old Sarina who was with her family on a bus at Walt Disney World in Florida. When a mixed-race family got on board, Sarina excitedly observed, "Look at that family—they're all different colors!" Neither Robby nor Sarina intended any harm. They simply could not perform the *cognitive* skill of putting themselves in another's place.

 **Essential**

> Instead of punishing a preschooler for saying something that may hurt someone else's feelings, talk to him about how what he said affected the other person. It won't build empathy if you punish your child for a skill that they cannot have at that point in their development.

A second part of empathy is being able to understand the other's perspective well enough to allow it to affect your actions, opinions, beliefs, or feelings. Go back to the game of hide and seek. If the two-year-old could take your perspective, she would probably change her behavior and choose a different hiding place. Four-year-old Sarina and five-year-old Robby may have chosen not to make their statements about others' characteristics if they possessed the ability to imagine what their statements would feel like from someone else's perspective.

As children age, they become *cognitively* able to take someone else's perspective, but their emotional self-centeredness (adults can have this too!) sometimes inhibits them from considering the other person's feelings or thoughts. For example, your eight-year-old may understand that you have a hurt leg and need to go to the doctor to get stitches, but balk at going with you because she wants to stay home and watch TV. Or, a pre-teen can cognitively understand your perspective about having a clean house, but still choose to leave his stuff lying around the family area because he forgets, doesn't want to be inconvenienced, or have to do tasks he believes are unimportant. This pre-teen is devoid of a critical part of empathy that is to *care about* the other person's perspective.

Let's suppose a child has both the cognitive skills to understand another's perspective and also cares about the other person's perspective. What happens then? Would a child or teen always be required to change an action, belief, or emotion? No, in fact, that could be unhealthy or lead to a bad decision. The pre-teen may cognitively understand why her friend dislikes a certain teacher and care that her friend is so distressed about this teacher. And, your pre-teen may spend time reading her friend's texts and reassuring her friend. But, empathy does not require your daughter to also dislike the teacher or even agree with some of the criticisms leveled by her friend. Empathy allows for the possibility—but does not require—that you alter your behaviors or emotions. It does require, however, that you understand and care about the other person's emotions in a way that will allow you to be understanding or supportive.

❓ Question

How is empathy different from sympathy?
Sympathy is an emotion you feel for someone else because of his misfortune or struggles. For example, if your child sees a homeless person on the street and talks about how cold the person must get at night, your child is demonstrating empathy. If your child simply says, "I feel sorry for him, can we give him a dollar?" it is a demonstration of sympathy.

Why Is Empathy Important?

Without the ability to empathize, your child will end up very self-centered, considering issues only from her perspective. Relationships will stall, job performance in adult life will suffer (is your opinion *always* the best one in a group?), and life will be devoid of a basic ability to connect with others.

 Alert

> Don't expect a three-year-old to say "I'm sorry" with any genuineness. Because he cannot take someone's perspective, the concept of emotionally offending or hurting someone else is beyond his understanding. Even so, you can explain to your child what he did to hurt someone else and require that he say "I'm sorry that I . . ." Make sure the child fills in what he did wrong (e.g., grabbed the toy from you) because this will help his development of empathy.

Empathy provides your child with choices. When she examines an issue from a friend's perspective, multiple options for different behavioral reactions become available. Think about the child described earlier who had accepted the overnight invitation from a friend only to find out her soccer team was going out for pizza after their 6 P.M. game. Empathy applied to this scenario would first cue your child to the fact that she should think about how her friend might react (some people don't even recognize the need to think about the other's perspective or they think it's irrelevant or unimportant compared to their own perspective). If your daughter decides to consider her friend's perspective, she'll likely realize that if she cancels or arrives late to spend the night, her friend will likely be disappointed (at best) or very offended, angry, or hurt (at worst). Once your daughter understands this perspective, then she can better weigh the consequences of her choice. Is this pizza outing so important to her that she's willing to disappoint her friend?

And, what would your daughter want the other child to do if the situation was reversed?

Stages of Empathy Development

Because empathy requires a certain level of cognitive skill, children possess different capacities for empathy at different ages. The newborn doesn't even realize that he's a person distinguishable from others, so therefore empathy is a moot point. By age two, the child is able to show empathy in limited circumstances. And by the teen years the only limit to empathy is that teens typically go through a form of adolescent egocentrism that can make empathy difficult.

Toddlers, Preschoolers, and Empathy

Your two-year-old will only be able to muster empathy for concrete actions that he can visually see or hear. For example, two-year-old Justin's mother banged her head while leaning in the car to buckle him into his seat. Her loud "Ouch" combined with grabbing her head made it easy for Justin to tell that she was hurt. He rubbed her face and said, "I make it better," an action that closely paralleled what his mother typically did in that situation. He will not, however, be equally empathic when it comes to the need to share a coveted toy. Why? Because that would require him to put himself in his friend's place and understand the frustration his friend probably feels. He doesn't yet have the cognitive capabilities to do that. And, he didn't do that with his mother's banged head either. He responded to her concrete actions by modeling what she typically did when he got hurt.

But, don't let preschool children's cognitive limitations discourage you from actively teaching empathy. If you directly model empathy by attuning to their emotions, teach them to apologize when they've done something wrong (make sure to emphasize others' emotional or physical hurt when you explain what your child did wrong), and ask them "what if" questions about characters in a story you are reading, they will have greater capacity for empathy once their cognitive skills catch up. Make it a habit to ask your child questions about characters in books. For example, take the classic *Goodnight Moon*, asking "Why do you think the child wanted to say goodnight to so many things?" promotes the cognitive skill of imaging what someone else is thinking or feeling. Real-life empathy comes more naturally the more it's practiced. Asking questions such as this alerts your daughter that paying attention to what others do and why they may be doing it is an important skill.

 **Essential**

Adult patience is required when dealing with the cognitive limitations that prevent empathy in toddlers. For example, a two-year-old was riding in her car seat in the back seat and pointed to something on the back seat that her mother could not see in the rearview mirror. "What's that?" the child kept saying with greater insistence. The mother finally stopped the car to get out and see what "that" was. It turned out to be a spider and the toddler was much relieved when her mother took care of it.

Empathy and Elementary School Children

Based on both cognitive development and emotional capacity, these are the golden years for teaching children to be empathic. Cognitively, they can now take someone else's perspective (physical or emotional) and emotionally, they don't have the egocentrism of a teenager. There are a myriad of opportunities each day to help your child develop empathy. Here are three ready sources of material. First, pay attention to your environment as you and your child move through the day. Maybe you see a wheelchair-bound person at the grocery store. Ask a simple question such as "What do you think would be the hardest part of being in a wheelchair all of the time?"

There's no right answer but any answer your child comes up with will have forced him to consider life from another person's point of view. You can do the same with news stories such as those about tornado or flood victims who lose their houses and all their possessions.

A second opportunity for empathy comes with the experiences of friends. Maybe a good friend's father was just laid off and now the family doesn't have as much money for the friend to do things like go to the movies. Helping your child think about others' hardships—or just about how things have changed for a family with a new baby or sick mother—will help develop empathy.

✅ Fact

> Humans engage in a reasoning error called the fundamental attribution error. This occurs whenever you attribute someone else's "bad" behavior to permanent personality characteristics (flaws), but excuse the same "bad" behavior in yourself because of situational factors. So the guy who pulled out in front of you is a "jerk" or "moron" but when you do this to others, you had to do it because traffic was so heavy and there weren't very many openings, so you did the best you could. Empathy would reduce this reasoning error; you'd assume others had a good reason as well.

A third opportunity for empathy development comes when your child is directly involved in a situation that requires her to be empathic, such as the child who has accepted the overnight invitation only to find out about her soccer team going out for pizza. You may question the use of the word "require" in the previous sentence. If all people considered empathy a requirement of human interaction—from loved ones, to friends, to a stranger in the mall—then people would reap benefits from stronger relationships to fewer crimes. Instead, some people seem to have been taught that considering someone else's perspective may harm or deprive them. Remember though, empathy does not require your daughter to skip the pizza party with her soccer team. But, if she chose to go to the pizza party, empathy would include something like asking the friend if they could get together on a different night or explaining to her friend why the pizza party is so important to her and letting her friend know she would like to arrive later. Empathy provides your daughter with additional information about someone else's perspective that she can then use to choose her course of action.

What Happens to Empathy in the Teen Years?

Empathy can seem to disappear from your pre-teen or teen's repertoire of behaviors. Teens experience a unique form of ego-centrism that makes them very self-focused. Even the most well-behaved and socially conscious teens must work their way through the stage where they believe that others are constantly watching them, creating self-consciousness and conformity. They must own the same phone, dress the same way, participate in the same activities, and so on because to be different sometimes means being an outcast. Unfortunately, this tendency to avoid being different or doing anything that draws unnecessary attention is one thing that contributes to bullies not being challenged by their peers. Your teen child has the *cognitive* capacity to understand what it must feel like to be the victim, but her high level of self-focus reduces her ability to *emotionally care* about what happens to the victim because she's using so much of her emotional energy to protect herself from the possibility of being the victim herself. Likewise, they don't care as much (emotionally) about issues that are important to parents—such as a clean room—because of this self-focus.

With more maturity, older teens tend to return to taking others' perspectives. They realize the universe does not revolve around them and thus are willing to use emotional resources to support others. And, when a teen leaves for college, empathy for parents can sometimes develop rapidly as they try to balance a full-time job (school) with chores (laundry, getting the oil changed, cleaning the toilet), exercise, fun, and enough sleep. How did their parents manage to do it?

 **Essential**

Try to help a teen understand your perspectives about curfews, safe driving, and such by asking questions that force the teen to think about you. For example, for a teen that is fighting a curfew, you might simply ask, "What reasons do you think I have for setting a curfew?" Instead of you talking, get the teen to verbalize your likely reasons.

Parenting Styles and Empathy

Two basic styles of parenting, authoritarian and authoritative, both influence empathy development. The authoritarian parent tends to be rule oriented, strict, and no nonsense. Parents make the decisions and children do what the parents want or they suffer the consequences. There's little room for discussing different points of view or differences of opinion. Authoritative parents, in contrast, are willing to have discussions with children—discussions that can help build empathy. Both styles of parenting involve setting high expectations for children, but the type of parent-child interaction in authoritative parenting makes it easier for the child to develop empathy.

Authoritarian Parenting and Empathy

The authoritarian style of parenting hampers empathy development because the style essentially communicates that only one perspective, the parent's, is relevant in any given situation. An authoritarian parent is typically unwilling to have discussions about rules, mutually problem solve about troublesome issues, and sometimes won't even allow a child to state an opinion. This style typically builds resentment in children as they move into their later childhood and teen years.

Authoritarian parents don't model empathy, so an unwritten rule in those families is that the only relevant perspective is the one of whoever is in charge. This sets children up to experience communication challenges in their own relationships and to see all conflict as a "win-lose" struggle rather than a win-win opportunity.

Authoritative Parenting and Empathy

Contrast the authoritarian style with the authoritative style and empathy development in children. First, authoritative parents do believe in discussion, particularly about problem issues—whether it's the child not cleaning her room or not completing her home-work. Instead of the "just do what I say" approach, the child of authoritative parents experiences the give and take of a discussion, the value of compromise, and the development of empathy. Her parents will be empathic with her—"we know you hate cleaning your room"—and expect her empathy in return. She's more likely to listen and understand your perspective when you say, "Nice clothes thrown on the floor can get damaged, candy wrappers and old sodas can attract bugs, and dust that builds up can create allergy problems. Plus it's important to us to have a clean house." Explanations such as this force the child to at least hear a perspective different from her own. Also, the empathy shown by the parent to the child builds a stronger relationship and a basis for possible compromise.

Consider the case of two-year-old Ali. Ali was ready to move from a crib to a bed. To make enough space in the room, a sofa had to be moved out. Ali's mom had shown her the new bed, where each piece of furniture would go once the bed was added, explained why the sofa needed to be moved, and so forth. Ali was excited about getting a "big girl bed" and had shown no resistance to the change. But, the day of the move, just as her dad and his friend had the big sofa angled to carry it through the doorway, Ali burst into tears. Clearly something was horribly wrong, but Ali was sobbing so hard that she couldn't talk. Her mom asked the guys to stop moving the sofa (not an easy task when it's halfway through the door) and pulled Ali onto her lap and gently asked, "What's wrong? What's upset you?" After several minutes of sobbing, Ali stopped crying and announced, "I know, Mommy, we'll go to the attic to read books." There it was—the reason for the sobs. Ali, because of her concrete reasoning, believed that if her sofa left the room, her parents would never read to her again. Ali loved to read books! Her mom, now able to understand why Ali was so upset, suggested they find a new spot in the bedroom to read. Ali pointed to her brand-new beanbag chair; it looked like the perfect place. They cuddled up to read a book while dad and his friend went back to the moving job.

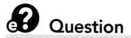 **Question**

Will my kids try to take advantage of me if I'm empathic with them?
That's highly unlikely and it really doesn't matter as long as you have the assertiveness you need to set appropriate boundaries. Authoritative parents set limits, have high expectations, and are willing to discuss issues with their kids. So, there's no reason to fear your children becoming spoiled just because you're willing to try to understand their thoughts and feelings.

Think about what Ali's mom gained by demonstrating empathy. First, she learned the reason for Ali's unhappiness and was able to address it right away. Of course they would still read! Of course she didn't want Ali to be concerned about that. But, the mother also gained more of her daughter's trust. Through this experience, Ali learned that she could show her true feelings and her mom and dad would try to understand those. No, she didn't always get her way, but neither did she have her feelings or perspective ignored.

Remember, empathy gives someone the opportunity to change a decision or take a different action, but it doesn't require that. The mother gained valuable information when she paused long enough to learn that Ali's distress centered on wanting to read. The sofa still got moved; that wasn't the issue.

Consider what Ali's mom probably would have done if she used an authoritarian style of parenting. First, she probably wouldn't have halted the moving. Instead, she would have told Ali this was the plan and reminded her that she knew about it. She would have been unlikely to ask Ali questions, most likely opting instead for commands such as "Stop crying." And, she wouldn't have helped Ali pick the new reading spot because she failed to explore Ali's reason for crying and didn't know the crying was related to a fear about not getting to read. The situation would have been somewhat resolved that night at bedtime when it was time to read books and they still read. In the meantime though, the parent had missed a golden opportunity to model empathy and to relieve understandable distress in her daughter.

Empathy builds understanding. A deeper understanding of what's wrong or what the other person thinks enables you to think about different options. And, having different options usually leads to a better solution and more people feeling satisfied.

CHAPTER 11

Social Responsibility

Social responsibility is demonstrated (or not) whenever your child is part of a group. Collaboration, cooperation, and thinking about others' well-being and what's good for the group, not just for herself, are all key characteristics of social responsibility. As your child grows older, the possibilities for behaving responsibly expand, such as thinking about the well-being of others at her school, in your community, and even in remote parts of the world. "What can I do to help?" and "What are my responsibilities to this group?" sum up this EI scale.

What Is Social Responsibility?

Does your child have to work to save the environment, protect endangered species, or help stop hunger to be socially responsible? Although all of these actions would qualify, they're a bit too removed from daily life for most kids. Instead, help your child see what he can do to help others within whatever groups he's a part of. The phrase social responsibility breaks down into words: "social" (with or for others) and "responsibility" (behaving with concern, respect, or commitment). Thus, you can begin teaching social responsibility to children as young as two. A two-year-old can understand simple things like taking a plate from the table to the sink helps other people. The word "help" or "helper" are very effective with two-year-olds. A five-year-old with more advanced cognitive skills can begin to understand the more complex notion that if there's a job to be done, five family members working together can get the job done much faster if they all work together. And as your child gets even older, it's possible to convey the sense that doing things to be helpful or cooperative adds value to him and the group.

Why Is Social Responsibility Part of Emotional Intelligence?

At first, social responsibility may seem more appropriate when applied to activism rather than children's emotional intelligence. An example may clarify why it's so important to teach social responsibility, which is the opposite of an "everything is all about me" attitude. Twelve-year-old Paige was invited by her mother to go to their church and serve dinner to the homeless families that were staying at the church for one week before rotating to another local church to stay there for a week. Host families (church members) volunteered to cook meals and provide some entertainment to the children of the homeless families. When Paige's mom first asked her about going along—Paige had just begun babysitting and liked children a lot—her response was fear. "Aren't you worried they'll hurt you?" she asked her mom.

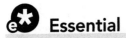 **Essential**

Social responsibility is an easy emotional intelligence skill to teach children because the opportunities are endless. Think about all of the things a child can do around the house or in the community to be helpful. Even something small—like holding a door open for someone who is carrying an armload of groceries—demonstrates social responsibility.

Where had Paige learned that homeless people harmed others? Most likely, it was a stereotype that Paige had acquired from listening to others talk about the homeless. Paige's mom talked her into going. As she played board games with the children, Paige asked them questions about school, sports, and other things. She quickly learned these kids were much like her except they didn't have a nice house, good clothes, and plenty of food. All of the parents were employed but most of them could not make ends meet after getting let go from a better-paying job. Homelessness was a temporary condition these families found themselves in due to a string of unfortunate circumstances.

As they drove home, Paige couldn't stop talking about how cute and friendly the kids were and how much their parents cared about them. Stereotype destroyed. She also expressed both sympathy ("I feel sorry for them that they don't have their own bed.") and empathy ("It must be hard not to be able to invite friends to your house or have a Christmas tree."). She then went one step further and asked her mom how soon they could volunteer again. She had gone from fear of the unknown, based on a stereotype, to a desire to help someone else in just one short hour. What a transformation. Emotionally intelligent people develop skills in working with a variety of people and understand the value of everyone in the community doing well.

Social responsibility teaches children to operate effectively in groups or teams, whether it's as part of a family, as a member of a sports team, or as a classmate. Very rarely do children or adults operate totally independently. Thus, learning how to skillfully collaborate and think about how to help the group succeed is a critical emotional intelligence skill because it will affect both relationship and work success.

Teaching Social Responsibility: There's No "I" in Team

The phrase, "There's no 'I' in team" is used by coaches and leaders to emphasize that when multiple people are involved, everyone should put the well-being of the team above (or at least on par with) her own well-being. In today's very competitive society with a focus on tangible measures of success—athletic feats, trophies or competitions won, high grades, getting into the best schools, or awards earned—social responsibility almost seems like it would work against your child achieving any of the previous measures of "success." Two examples, one related to academics and the other to athletics, may help dispute that view.

✅ Fact

Children who have played competitive, team-oriented sports have been shown to work more effectively in teams within the workplace as adults because they are used to relying on others and being relied on, accepting responsibility for mistakes, and understanding everyone's contribution.

Academic Success

Imagine your child is a star math student and the classroom teacher wants to use a technique called peer learning. You may balk at the fact that your child is asked to spend time helping another child learn the math rather than being challenged with new material herself. After all, it's the latter that will best prepare her for **her** future. So, why should you support her helping someone with less skill level?

Let's examine this situation a bit more closely. First, if you've ever had to teach material to someone else, you're aware that you have to master the material at an even higher level in order to effectively teach it. So, your child would benefit academically from helping a peer learn. Then there's also the reality of today's classroom. With children of so many different ability levels, it benefits the whole class to help the less gifted master the material more quickly. This allows the class to move forward into new material sooner than it otherwise would have, which also benefits your child. And, the reality is that most schools will find a way to provide extra stimulation and academic enrichment to any child who is academically talented.

So, parents can benefit from reframing their thoughts from a focus just on their child, to how helping the whole group move ahead also benefits their child. And, it benefits your child in non-academic ways as well. Think about Paige and her reaction to homeless people. Interacting with others you know less about can serve as a powerful and positive learning experience that will undoubtedly benefit your child, helping her become less judgmental, more caring, and more effective at working with lots of different types of people—attitudes and skills that will foster her future success.

 Essential

Research demonstrates that the best way to overcome a prejudice or stereotype about someone is to work with them toward a common goal. Working together forces people to get to know each other as people. For a great movie that teaches this lesson, watch the movie *Remember the Titans*.

Athletic Success

Suppose your ten-year-old is a star basketball player and has been invited to participate on a club team that practices almost daily and travels out of town to games. Your child plays the point-guard position. Another child on the same club team also plays point guard and is not as skilled as your child. Yet, the coach plays your child about 60 percent of the time and the other child about 40 percent of the time. And, he does that even when games are close and it could cost your team a victory. Furthermore, the coach assigns the two point guards to work on drills with each other in practice. So, instead of your child getting to do the drills with another "starter" or first-team player, he's working with someone who could take over his position as a starter if the other child becomes more skilled. Isn't that going too far?

Again, examine this from a different perspective. First, assume that the roles were reversed and your child is the second-string player. You'd be thrilled at all the coach is doing to help your child develop. You'd probably even describe the coach to your friends as "fair, someone who cares about all the kids getting to play and developing their skills" or something similar. The coach hasn't changed anything, but he's gone from villain to hero depending on your child's skill level. Maybe you're scratching your head now, thinking something such as "well, that's just the way the world works, some people are more skilled than others and they should reap the rewards of that." Living by this logic results in what some call the "haves" and the "have nots," a situation that typically creates more conflict and consequences for everyone involved, even the "haves." (You only need to look at crime rates in industrialized countries to understand the impact of crime on the entire society, not just the criminals.) Also, keep in mind the children in question are only ten years old.

In case you're still not convinced the coach should play the other child so much and give him an equal opportunity in practice, there's a second way to frame this situation. Suppose your child is the starter, plays the whole game except when he gets in foul trouble or his team is leading by a wide margin at the end of the game. And, during practice, your child does drills exclusively with other first-team players.

Your child's team has made it to the regional playoffs and if they win two games, they go to the state level. They win the first game but overnight your child develops a serious virus. He's vomiting, running a fever of 102°F and crying because he feels so miserable. He can't play today. So the back-up point guard, the one with very little game experience and not as many opportunities to develop in practice, must play the whole game. He does okay but makes critical defensive mistakes and doesn't score nearly as much as your child would have and the team loses. This second-string player (child) feels miserable enough, but that's made even worse when he overhears comments from some parents in the stands about his level of skill. After the game, the first-team players ignore him (after all, they've been conditioned by the coach to believe the second-string players are unimportant).

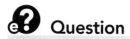 ## Question

What should a parent do if his child is the second-string player and the coach does not provide opportunities to develop?
The answer depends somewhat on the circumstances such as age of your child, whether the coach could be fired for losing "too much" and other similar factors. You can always, however, empathize with your child's frustration and ask her what she would do differently to help all players develop? Connect her responses to social responsibility—thinking about the well-being of the larger group rather than just yourself.

So, not only does one child feel miserable, but the whole team is denied a chance to play for the state title. Your son clearly loses something in this situation. So does everyone on the team. Now imagine how you would feel if your son had been the second-string player in this scenario, the one whom everybody is criticizing. Think about it. Which model of "team" is more effective for everyone on the team, both in terms of winning and in terms of respect and cooperation? You can't have it both ways, leaving the second-stringers behind when your child is on the first team and then wanting second-stringers to have a reasonable chance to develop when your child is on the second team. If you do desire both of those scenarios, you are unwittingly teaching your child "It's all about me," an attitude that will clearly come back to haunt him in work and personal relationships throughout life.

There are two valuable lessons to be learned; first, everyone on a team has a role to play and deserves to be seen as an equally valuable member of the team. This does not mean they are all equally skilled or will play equal amounts of time. But how are they viewed by the coach, other teammates, and parents in the stands—as someone who deserves respect and contributes to the level of his talent, or as someone who costs your child playing time because the coach is trying to be nice? Second, sooner or later, every member of the team will need to perform in some way to help the team. The child who got sick with the bad virus would have been well enough to play for the championship. But, he didn't get that chance because the second-string point guard wasn't prepared to play in a game that mattered. Or, the contribution of second-team players who feel respected and a part of the team may be to practice really hard, not only to develop their skills, but also provide a better challenge for the first-team players in practice.

Teaching Social Responsibility: The Dreaded Chores

One of the age-old conflict areas between parents and children revolves around doing chores. Whether you've tried chore charts, designated times for chores, positive reinforcement, punishment, or any number of other tactics, getting children to do chores is a constant struggle in many families. Perhaps you need to frame the reason for doing chores in a way that helps your child understand *why* this is an obligation and a sign of respect for other family members.

Here's how to start. When your children are very young, begin with basic chores such as picking up their toys after play, and when they are old enough, carrying their dirty plates to the kitchen sink. Instead of focusing on the end result—a clean table—focus on *why* your child should want to help. Your conversation may go something like this with a three-year-old.

Dad: You need to pick up your toys now.

Son: No, don't want to.

Dad: I understand. Cleaning up isn't nearly as much fun as messing things up or playing. (Notice the empathy.)

Son: (Many children probably won't say anything because they're used to the parent just restating the command.)

Dad: Here's why Mom and I want you to clean up. We're all part of the family. So, each one of us has to help with the "work" that must be done in the family. That's a respectful way to treat each other.

Son: Okay.

Dad: And, if you clean up your messes, that means Mom and I have more free time to spend playing or reading with you.

Son: Okay.

Dad: So, I need you to put your toys away. Let me know if you need help.

This conversation emphasizes that within a group, the family in this case, all group members need to contribute up to their ability level because it helps everyone in the group, including the individual. More time for parent-child interaction and less conflict benefit everyone in the family.

When you ask (or require) your child to do something to help the group, frame it in terms of how everyone benefits, including your child. It's no wonder that children resist chores—again, chores are not fun—when the only reasons they may be given are "do it because I said so" or "do it because we need a clean floor."

Even saying, "do it because we all have chores" still misses the essence of social responsibility which is focused on thinking about the well-being of the group.

𝒆❓ Question

Does paying children for chores diminish the lessons of social responsibility?
Yes, it does. All children should have chores for which they are not paid; they're expected to do these to contribute their part to help the family group. Beyond that though, if a child wants to earn extra money by doing additional chores, pay them! They're showing initiative and likely saving you time.

If children are learning the lessons of social responsibility, they'll eventually start doing things to help you or the entire family without you having to ask. For example, the ten-year-old may load his younger sister's dishes in the dishwasher or the twelve-year-old may voluntarily reorganize her closet, getting rid of clothes that her younger sister may want. As teens, children with high social responsibility begin to learn more of the mutuality required in relationships, another aspect of social responsibility. If the teen wants to borrow a parent's car and not have to pay for the gas, she's benefiting from being a member of that family. She may, in turn, readily agree to watch her younger siblings (without pay) while her parents go out for a "date night." Instead of things being based on a quid pro quo system, actions are taken out of recognition that if we all work together, we'll all benefit.

Teaching Social Responsibility: Community Spirit

Must your child engage in community service to develop her social responsibility? Learning to care about the well-being of others that you may not otherwise come in contact with certainly sharpens your social responsibility skills. But, you don't have to take five hours each Saturday cleaning up a local highway.

Cooperate, Help

Some of the simplest ways social responsibility manifests itself is by cooperating with others' requests. Suppose your child's teacher asks for a volunteer to stay inside during recess to help set up an activity for later that day. Volunteering to help with that task demonstrates social responsibility. Yes, your child may be giving up something he would prefer, but he's learning that helping others accomplish their goals can be rewarding as well.

When you're out in public with your child, you'll have numerous opportunities to teach social responsibility. You could be in a mall parking lot and observe a young mother struggle to manage a baby in a stroller, a two-year-old who doesn't want to hold her hand, and multiple packages stacked on top of the stroller. You can model social responsibility by helping this young mother get to her car.

Fact

A well-studied concept in psychology termed "bystander assistance" shows that people are less likely to help others when multiple people are around (surely someone else will help) and when they're scared of getting involved (too much time, may be asked to do more, etc.).

Once inside the mall, you may observe a harried worker who is trying to sort through dozens of shirts and pants that have been left in disarray by other shoppers. Teaching your child to fold the shirt and put it back in the correct place (or whatever the store asks you to do with clothes you've tried on) demonstrates cooperation. You enter another store and notice a dad with his five-year-old and they seem to be in a hurry. The son accidentally bumps into a display and fifty watches go tumbling to the floor. The exasperated father pauses and you offer to help him pick up the watches. He thanks you and notes they're in a hurry to get to a long-awaited birthday party and he's running late because his other child got sick this morning. The watches are picked up quickly with both children helping.

🅴❗ Alert

Because children imitate TV characters, it's important to manage what your children watch. They're likely to increase in social responsibility if they watch shows that actively teach or model social responsibility, also sometimes referred to as prosocial behavior. But, they can also pick up behaviors that lack social responsibility.

Why don't more people stop to offer such forms of help? One reason may be a form of selfishness: you assume your time is more valuable or your next activity is more important than the other person's. Or, since you didn't cause the problem, there's no obligation to help. If this is what you model for your kids, this is what they'll learn. And not only may they fail to stop and help someone else, they may walk away from a mess they caused because of the belief that their time or agenda is more important than others' or that others are being paid to clean up the mess so there's no need to stop. Again, reverse the roles. How would you want others to treat you or your child if you were the ones that needed help?

Think about how this more self-oriented view of the world may play out as your child goes to college and begins a career. She may be terribly ineffective at group projects because she doesn't respond to e-mails (she prefers text messages and expects others to adapt because she's busy), doesn't really have time to meet, doesn't do her share of the work (she believes she has a heavier course load so it's okay if she doesn't do her fair share), or cannot readily come to a compromise with other team members because she wants to do things her way. Will this child grow into an adult who suddenly becomes effective at collaborating and cooperating with others in the workplace or with a spouse? Employers today indicate that teamwork is one of the most important skills for college graduates to possess, yet some graduates lack this skill. And, spouses generally aren't receptive to doing all of the work while the partner does little. Undeveloped teamwork skills have consequences!

Giving and Volunteering

Giving time or material possessions to others is a critical part of social responsibility development. There are many different ways and different times of year to teach children to give. During the November and December holiday season, there are multiple and easy ways to give. Names of children from needy families and what they would like for Christmas or Hanukkah are easy to find. Ask your child to contribute 10 to 20 percent of his allowance to buy a gift for another child who has asked for something like a warm winter coat. Or, call your local social service office and find out if you can cook a meal or buy groceries for another family. Involve your child in the cooking and shopping. Or, take your family to the local soup kitchen to serve warm food to homeless people on a cold night. None of these activities requires a heavy time commitment, yet all of them teach a child how to be a collaborative member of his community.

 **Essential**

An easy way to teach children about social responsibility is to have them clean out their closets and toy areas once a year, giving away old clothes and toys to a local Goodwill store. Take the child with you to deliver the items and explain what will happen to the donated items.

Some forms of community service, such as building a Habitat for Humanity house, are easy to measure in terms of the impact of your contribution. Others may be harder to measure such as helping clean up a roadside when it's likely that it will soon be littered again. But, when drivers see people picking up the trash, that deters them from littering. And, a clean highway leading into your community fosters greater pride (the good kind) and sense of shared responsibility for helping the community stay vibrant and an attractive place to live. It's very important for you, as the parent, to talk about the benefits of giving and serving, both to the recipients and for your child.

Alert

More well-developed empathy makes it easier for children to understand the perspectives and emotions of the people they help or serve. Without empathy, participating in socially responsible activities may be done without excitement, satisfaction, or learning. The child would be going through the motions but not benefiting personally.

Clubs and Organizations, School Requirements

Children and teens who participate in groups that take on any kind of service project or community work benefit in multiple ways. First, they receive the satisfaction of helping and often see tangible benefits of their work (e.g., a completed Habitat House, smiling elderly people at the nursing home). And, they are typically exposed to issues such as homelessness that they've never thought about much before. This involvement broadens their perspective, much the way that Paige's visit with the homeless families staying at her church broadened her perspective. Children then learn to think more critically (not as in critical, but rather as more systematically and thoroughly) about all of the issues involved in homelessness, realizing that it's not so easy to dismiss all homeless people as lazy or seeking a free handout. This increase in critical reasoning is one reason why more than half of all public high schools in the United States either require or provide community service opportunities to their students: the growth in cognitive development can be just as powerful as the benefits of being socially responsible.

CHAPTER 12

Reality Testing

T he lack of effective reality testing skills may carry some of the most significant personal consequences compared with all other areas of emotional intelligence. Why? If a child doesn't know to scan the environment for information that may be helpful, and/or misreads the information by either under- or over-reacting to it, the consequences can be very serious. Reality testing may be a concept you've never heard of, but teaching your child skills in this area are essential to her short- and long-term success.

What Is Reality Testing?

Reality testing incorporates two different skill sets. First, your child needs to be curious and seek information rather than be passive. For example, your fourth grader who got an average grade on a science project will benefit if she's curious enough to read the teacher's comments about the grade and go talk to the teacher to get more feedback. Too often though, both parents and children are guilty of looking at the grade only, often missing key information that could contribute to longer-term success.

A second element of reality testing involves calibrating your response to the information collected, neither over- nor under-reacting. Consider the science project example. Assume the teacher advised that the project needed to be better organized and the findings clearly stated. An over-reaction to the feedback may go something like this: crying, complaining about the teacher's unfair grading or unclear instructions, or your child deciding that science isn't his strength. All of those are over-reactions. Children haven't had much experience with big projects by fourth grade so it's best to frame the project as a chance to learn new skills and the feedback as a tool to help him in the future. If you've heard the saying "make a mountain out of a mole hill," that may help you understand what over-reacting to feedback may look like.

Under-reacting to the feedback is just as damaging. Suppose your child dismisses the feedback as overly critical or not fair and turns down an opportunity to meet with the teacher. Sometimes, the under-reaction takes the form of "she doesn't like me," deflecting the responsibility to the teacher. Under-reaction often takes the form of denial (e.g., she really didn't give me any helpful feedback), dismissal of the importance (e.g., science projects are rare, therefore there's no need to worry about this), or blaming others (e.g., another teacher would have graded the project better, so there's no need to try to improve). Under-reacting fails to acknowledge the problem and thus it's likely to reoccur; there will be other projects where your child struggles with organization or with communicating findings in a clear and concise way.

 Fact

A concept called *locus of control* explains whether your child tends to take responsibility for her actions—both "successes" and "failures"—or whether she looks to external factors such as whether someone else likes her, bad luck, or getting a really hard teacher. Teaching your child to accept responsibility will help her develop better reality testing.

Why Is Reality Testing Important?

Good reality testing equips your child to successfully navigate a variety of situations both safely and with a level of reaction that the situation requires. You cannot cover every possible situation your child may encounter, but you can teach your child to be both curious and then calibrated in her responses. Curiosity will help your child ask the right questions or explore information that already exists and is important to think about, and calibration will enable her to react with just the right amount of intensity or the best behavioral choices, neither over- nor under-reacting.

For example, let's say your five-year-old wants to jump off the high diving board at the local swim club. He's not particularly fond of heights, but all of his friends are jumping off. A child who asks a friend, "Was it scary up that high?" is seeking information that will help him decide. Suppose the friend said, "Real scary, it looks much higher up there." Now your child has to decide how to use that information. Will he ignore it, thus under-reacting and telling himself he won't be scared (even though he's already scared or he would have already made the jump!) or will he over-react and decide he's never going to jump off the high dive? A more calibrated response might be to practice jumping off the lower diving board a lot and then try jumping off the high board. Another way to calibrate the response is to ask a parent to stand at the bottom part of the ladder. And yet another way to calibrate the response is to wait a month and see if he's less scared.

At the most basic level, reality testing could be a safety issue. While parents protect children from dangers during their younger years, as children become increasingly independent, there are more times when parents are not around. Suppose your child goes over to another child's house to play. You're unaware that the father in that family has a gun collection. Your child's friend wants to show your son his dad's guns. You get the picture. You'd want your child to ask himself the question, "Could this be dangerous?" and then react accordingly.

 Alert

Many everyday events could (theoretically) be dangerous. Riding in a car, crossing the street, or leaving the stove on *could* be dangerous. The goal with reality testing is not to exacerbate anxiety or create hermits; rather, the goal is to teach children to seek and weigh information before acting, rather than ignoring it.

Consider this true story. Some seven-year-olds were playing outside on a hot summer day. Two of them ran inside to get some ice. As they ran back outside, one of them suggested that they throw some ice cubes at their friends from the deck. They did, and one of the cubes hit another child just at the corner of her eye, causing her to need five stitches. They were all very lucky the flying cube did not hit the child's eye. While this action may also have involved some problems with impulse control, excellent reality testing would have stopped the kids from throwing the ice because they would have asked themselves, "Is this a good idea?" and then thought about the possible consequences. But, they didn't show enough "curiosity" or willingness to take in information. And, their impulses led to a bad decision, which is why impulse control is part of the decision-making area of emotional intelligence.

Take another issue. If your nine-year-old is repeatedly getting bullied on the bus ride home, it's ineffective reality testing for your child to assume it will just stop or that the bullying won't hurt him. But, many kids make that decision and don't tell the parents about the bullying, partly fueled by poor reality testing and partly because their self-regard has been scathed by the bullying. Or, they don't tell you because they don't realize you could have important information to teach them about how to make it stop (the "curiosity" factor). Parents, working effectively with schools, can stop bullying and so your child would be making a harmful (to himself) decision to under-react to getting bullied.

Parenting Styles and Reality Testing Skills

Back to parenting styles—your style will be part of what determines whether your child develops good reality testing or not. Remember the authoritarian parent who demands instant obedience and is not typically willing to provide explanations or discuss issues with the child? The authoritative parent, in contrast, is willing to explain, answer questions, and even discuss other options with children. The discussion-oriented behaviors are associated with better development of reasoning skills because the child gets lots of practice and the parents are constantly modeling how to reason through situations.

Consider this example of a likely authoritarian versus authoritative parental response to an issue. Eight-year-old Sam is unexpectedly invited to a classmate's birthday party on a Saturday in the fall. The family had already planned to go to some nearby mountains for a day of hiking. Sam begs his parents to go to the party instead and then go home with a friend after the party until his parents and older sisters (ten and twelve) return from the hike. A conversation between an *authoritarian* parent and a child might go like this:

Sam: Mom, can I go to Matt's party?

Mom: If it's on Saturday, no, you can't go. You know we planned a hiking trip.

Sam: But I don't want to go hiking, I want to go to the party.

Mom: Well, you're not going to the party; it's a family outing.

Sam: But we have lots of family outings. Can't I just miss this one?

Mom: No; now stop asking me to change my mind. You're going hiking with us.

Even though Sam's Mom engages in conversation, Sam is never given a reason other than, it's a family outing and he's expected to participate.

Now, look at the same scenario replayed with an *authoritative* parent.

Sam: Mom, can I go to Matt's party?
Mom: When is it?
Sam: Saturday afternoon.
Mom: That's in the middle of when we were going hiking as a family.
Sam: I'd rather go to the party.
Mom: Tell me why this party is so important to you. (Mom is showing empathy, asking a question to try to understand his perspective.)
Sam: All my friends were invited and they're taking us to play laser tag! I don't want to miss that.
Mom: Sounds like fun. How will you feel about missing the hike? You and your Dad had talked about jumping off that rock into the spring water.
Sam: I know, but I really want to go to the party. Can we go hiking Sunday afternoon?
Mom: Let me check with your Dad to see if he has anything planned for Sunday. I need you to check with your sisters about switching to Sunday.
Sam: If they can't switch days, can I still go to the party?
Mom: Let's wait to see what we find out from your dad and sisters before we start talking about that.
Sam: Okay.

There's a decision to make here. Does Sam get to go the party or not? You may think that's the parent's decision to make, not Sam's. Even if you believe that, you would be missing a prime opportunity to teach reality testing if you simply said "no." First, you'd be missing a chance to teach Sam to collect important and relevant information before making a decision. Part of making good decisions is to think about what types of information you need (again, the curiosity part). Second, there's no opportunity to weigh the information collected if you don't seek that information. Part two of reality testing involves looking at the information collected and reacting to it appropriately, neither under- nor over-reacting. Children miss the opportunity to weigh the pros and cons, consider various facts and rank their importance, and learn other reasoning skills if the parent simply says "no."

🄴❓ Question

Are you modeling effective reality testing?
Let your children hear you discussing the pros and cons of a decision or what additional information you need before you can make a decision. Help them understand the importance of being thoughtful and probing.

The authoritative mother did several things in this conversation to encourage Sam's reality testing. First, she provided him with information that he may not be thinking about—the family hiking trip—because he's so excited about the birthday party. That's pretty normal eight-year-old behavior. Once he has that information, Sam still "ranks" going to the birthday party ahead of going hiking. Mom then does a second thing to help him build reality testing—she asks him to explain why the party is so important. It's clear from his answer that playing laser tag with friends ranks above hiking.

But, that should not be the end of the discussion. His mom then provides him with additional information, reminding him that he and his dad had planned to jump off a rock into the spring water. This new information helps him realize that he does want to go hiking. That prompts him to be curious—to ask a question that will give them even more information. Is it possible to go on Sunday? Mom and Sam agree to collect that information.

Sam reports back that his sisters are fine with switching to Sunday, but his dad had a golf game scheduled. Could he switch the game to Saturday, Sam inquired? No, because he had already tried to set up a Saturday game of golf and couldn't find anyone; that was one reason they had set the hiking for Saturday and golf for Sunday. Now Sam has even more information to weigh. Teaching him to think about all of it and working through it in discussion form (rather than immediately telling him he cannot go to the party) will build his reality testing skills. And, through discussion, Sam might share additional information about why the party is so important. Maybe he's been trying to make friends with Matt and this invitation shows he's succeeded. But, if the discussion is short-circuited, the parent won't have considered all the information and neither will the child. There is not one "right" answer to this dilemma or for many of the other decisions you face in life. The answer will vary based on family priorities and what information emerges during the discussion.

Discipline Techniques and Reality Testing

Two commonly used discipline techniques—natural consequences and logical consequences—help boost children's reality testing ability. *Natural consequences* occur naturally in cause-effect situations without any need for parental intervention. For example, refusing to eat any part of dinner would result in hunger. Your child will be tired the next day if she stays up too late. Not doing homework results in a lower grade. Throwing a toy down during a tantrum could result in the toy getting broken. Leaving your jacket at school could mean your child experiences a cold ride home on the bus. Don't protect your child from natural consequences unless they involve health or safety issues. For example, letting a child run into the street to teach them traffic safety is foolish. But, letting them be hungry, cold, or tired will not damage their health or safety and typically the learning occurs quickly!

Logical consequences involve situations where the parent must intervene but the discipline technique is relevant to the misbehavior. Suppose, for example, your child is supposed to walk the family dog immediately after coming home from school. She forgets and the dog pees inside. Guess who should clean up that mess? If you want to teach reality testing, your daughter should clean it up to your satisfaction. As you supervise the clean-up, stay neutral and do not become punitive or say things like, "I told you so." Your insistence on a consequence that logically relates to the misbehavior will teach a child a valuable lesson. She cannot ignore "facts" or information simply because it's not convenient for her to pay attention to them. Ignoring her puppy that was prancing at her feet brought some logical consequences. Taking toys away from a three-year-old who refuses to clean up means he doesn't have those favorite toys to play with for the next three days.

In general, discipline techniques that are based in reason and discussion are far more effective than techniques that involve withdrawal of love or assert power through physical punishment. Why? Because reason-based techniques help the child learn from his mistakes and focus on the situation rather than the punishment.

How much discussion should you engage in when using natural and logical consequences? A lot! Explain that behaviors produce certain consequences (positive, negative, neutral) and that she needs to be alert and ask herself questions before engaging in a behavior, which is the curiosity part of reality testing. A question such as "What will happen if I don't do my homework?" helps the child face reality instead of pretending it doesn't matter or even exist.

Discuss the consequences of spending an entire allowance the first day the child receives it and then let the child experience the consequences if she chooses to do so anyway! Later in the week when she asks for money to buy something, gently remind her she made a decision earlier and now she needs to live with that decision. If you rescue your child, and that's very tempting to do, you deny her the chance to test reality.

Take this example of three-year-old Wyatt. His parents had long tried to have a child and could not. In their late thirties, they were able to adopt Wyatt and were thrilled to finally be parents. They enrolled him in a high-quality child care center run by the university where both of his parents were professors. The parents requested a meeting one day with the center director (also a professor) and one of the graduate teaching assistants who worked in the center. Wyatt's parents were beside themselves. Although reports from the center indicated he ate a variety of foods at lunch without complaint, each night at home he refused to eat dinner and demanded a hamburger. Each night the parents vowed they would not give in and a power struggle ensued.

 Alert

Avoiding the temptation to rescue children is very hard. So, make a list of situations where you're tempted to rescue (homework, money, bed time, cleaning up) and then what you can do to avoid rescuing. This will increase the chances that the child will learn from her mistakes rather than count on you to make things right.

If Wyatt's parents had been willing to let the natural consequence of hunger take its course, Wyatt would have eaten dinner. But each night before bed, they gave into his cries of hunger, sometimes even rushing out to the grocery store to buy hamburger meat! They knew this wasn't the best thing to do but needed validation that letting him go without dinner for a few nights would not harm him. That night at dinner, they explained that if he didn't eat his dinner, then he would get hungry and they would not give him anything else. But, they had said this many times before and never let him go hungry. Tonight would be different, they vowed.

As expected, Wyatt did not eat his dinner. At about eight o'clock, he began crying because he was hungry. The crying lasted for two hours, most of it fueled by anger (his parents had changed the rules on him!), not by hunger. His mom had to leave the house she got so distressed. A little after ten o'clock, the crying ceased and Wyatt fell asleep. The next morning he awoke and ate a huge breakfast. That night he again refused to eat dinner and this time he cried for about forty-five minutes, at first because he was hungry. The next morning he awoke very hungry and eagerly consumed his breakfast. By night three, Wyatt ate about half the food on his plate. Before bed, he asked for something to eat and his parents gently reminded him that he had chosen not to eat his dinner (all food they knew he liked from what he ate at the day care center) and that if you choose not to eat, you get hungry. The fourth night and thereafter, Wyatt ate his dinner without complaint or request for a hamburger. Getting really hungry had given him a huge dose of reality testing!

Other Strategies for Teaching Reality Testing

An authoritative parenting style and using logical and natural consequences as discipline techniques work because they share a common strategy of *discussion* based on facts and relevant other information. Those strategies also teach children to think more broadly about their behaviors and what they may need to consider that they have not yet considered.

Children's Games

Some children's games involve making decisions that have consequences. If you spend too much for a property, you may become bankrupt and lose a game. If you pick the wrong room to go into, someone may solve the crime before you do. If you take over the wrong country or maneuver your ships into a dangerous location, you may lose a war. In one popular board game children get to choose whether to go to college, have kids, what their occupation will be, and a whole host of other decisions that mimic adult reality. And, they experience the consequences (some positive, some negative) of their choices. Playing games that call for decision-making and have consequences provides a great way to discuss reality testing.

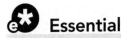 **Essential**

Younger children tend to like to "cheat" at these games because they want to win. It would be better to find ways to help them win that are based in reality—good decisions, smart strategy, and so on. So, there are two reasons not to look the other way when your preschooler cheats—teaching her a value (honesty) and helping her experience reality (sometimes you lose, better strategies produce better outcomes, and so on).

Television Shows and Books

Another strategy is to talk about TV or book characters. If a character rushed into a situation without collecting information, ask your child what the character should have asked himself. Also, look for situations where someone over- or under-reacts to information. The character who believes "no one likes me" because of one fight with a good friend is over-reacting. You can also teach your child to "think ahead" by asking (before you turn the page or before the commercial ends), "What do you think will happen next?" This type of question helps children practice connecting one behavior to another or to a likely consequence, either of which boosts their reality testing.

Events

You can use things that happen to other people as a basis for reality testing. Someone who refuses to leave home is under-reacting when a mandatory evacuation is ordered because of a category five hurricane. This belief that "bad things won't happen to me" or "it won't be as bad as they are predicting," results in lots of miscalculations and even fatal outcomes.

 Fact

Preschool children tend to be very concrete in their reasoning, sometimes assigning cause and effect because two things happen to occur simultaneously. For example, a four-year-old can become ter-rified of going to bed if a baby brother died of Sudden Infant Death Syndrome because "beds cause you to die." So, be aware that they tend to create cause and effect where it doesn't exist. You'll need to show them concrete examples of the opposite event to overcome the faulty reasoning.

Less consequential events also can be used to teach reality testing. If your four-year-old child refuses to share toys with a friend who is invited for a play date, the friend may end up crying or ask-ing to go home early. Your seven-year-old who forgets to put his bike in the garage and leaves it at the bottom of the driveway has a bike covered in mud after a big rainstorm. The more you point out the connection between decisions and consequences, the more your child will develop strong reality testing skills.

CHAPTER 13

Problem Solving

Even infants need and display problem-solving skills! Suppose your five-month-old cannot crawl and a toy is just out of reach. The toy is perched on the edge of a blanket that your child can reach. So, she may grab the blanket and pull. Or, she may begin wailing and expect you to understand what she wants. The latter example summarizes an important part of problem solving—emotions. Good problem solving accounts for how emotions are affecting you, which then helps you leverage emotions to help you rather than letting them derail you.

What Is Problem Solving?

Problem solving is a multistep process. Most experts describe a process that involves six or seven stages or steps, beginning with the ability to *recognize a problem exists.* Then, you must *accurately define the problem,* which can be harder than it seems. Why? Because your emotions get in the way and cloud your thinking! Once a problem is accurately defined and your emotions accounted for, *seeking information* that would help produce a better solution may be required. Next comes *brainstorming (identifying) possible solutions.* After solutions are identified, *evaluating them and choosing one* to implement is the next stage. Finally, *evaluating the effectiveness of the solution implemented* is required. If the latter step does not occur, then an ineffective solution can stay in place indefinitely. A better strategy would be to go back and try a different solution if the first one did not work well.

 Alert

One of the best indicators of whether you have problem-solved effectively is whether the problem has gone away. If it hasn't gone away, you'll need to come up with a different solution or perhaps do a better job of implementing the solution you chose.

Why Is Problem Solving Important?

Can you imagine living a satisfying life without good problem-solving skills? No matter the age, most people are confronted with multiple problems each day. Thankfully, many are small and barely register in your brain before a solution is implemented. But other problems can have enormous consequences and the failure to use an effective process that builds logically from one step to the next will almost guarantee ineffective outcomes.

Problem solving has another benefit as well. Both reality testing and problem solving share the advantage of teaching your child better reasoning skills, a gift that will aid them in school, at work, and in relationships.

 **Essential**

One of the hallmarks of effective problem solving is that the process of finding a solution involves the affected people. So, if you tend to solve problems for your child without her input, she may not be very invested in making that solution work.

Another benefit of teaching your child problem-solving skills is that it requires your child to be more attuned to his emotions and how they are affecting him at any given time. The more emotional self-awareness your son possesses, the better he will navigate most situations in life.

A final benefit of problem solving is that you can use it to teach your child the art of compromise and how to look for "win-win" solutions rather than "win-lose" solutions.

A Detailed Look at Problem Solving

Suppose your six-year-old child has become a balky eater. You could try a multitude of strategies, including allowing her to experience the natural consequences of hunger. Maybe you prefer to make this a different type of learning experience though, so you invite your child to engage in problem solving with you. Here's how that might look.

Recognizing a Problem Exists

You know a problem exists—she's not eating enough high nutrient foods—but how can you get a six-year-old to recognize that? Getting her to recognize this as a problem will be a key to reaching a good solution. Different strategies will work for different children, but here's one you may want to try. Explain to her that her body needs a certain amount of healthy food for her to grow effectively. So, if she wants to be as tall as her mom, as strong as her older sister, or a better dancer (fill in something important to your child), she must eat healthy foods. Or, it could simply be a family requirement that everyone eats a certain amount of food from each food group every day, including the parents! If she's not doing this then she's violating a family agreement or rule. Regardless of your approach, she needs to understand or agree that her picky eating is a problem.

Understand the Emotions Involved

Both parents and kids can experience strong emotions around the topic of food. For example, the parents' frustration may grow and grow the pickier the child is. And the child's frustration probably grows as well, especially when forced to eat foods she doesn't like. Soon, both the parent and child become angry and the problem escalates. When going through the steps of problem solving, it's important to stay attuned to how your emotions are driving your thinking and how her emotions are driving her thinking. If you are fearful that her picky eating will mean she doesn't progress as fast in dancing, it's critical that you are aware of that emotion because otherwise, your anxiety may drive you to different solutions, ones that may increase the problem rather than resolve it.

Teach her to be attentive to her emotions as well. Maybe she gets mad when you try to force her to eat everything on her plate. Her anger will intensify as you become more adamant. Or, she could become more resolute about not eating the more you choose different solutions without her involvement. You can get stuck in a vicious cycle and the problem doesn't get resolved.

If you're thinking something like, "I'm the parent and I know what's best, so why should I negotiate this," consider the implications of that approach. Unless you're willing to literally force the food into her mouth, you would most likely have to place severe consequences on a failure to eat or add significant rewards for eating healthy things. If you choose the punishment approach, emotions could rapidly escalate, leaving everybody mad, frustrated, and possibly emotionally wounded. If you offered a reward, you would have to make it big enough to make her want to eat foods she doesn't like. That may require more than is reasonable when there are other, more practical and effective, solutions.

And, if she has a limited palate, the option of letting her go hungry day after day simply isn't a good option. So, you'll need to examine what's most important to you—getting your child to eat better or controlling her behavior. You'd be better served by using a problem-solving approach that takes into account emotions, and lets you exercise parental wisdom and guidance while still getting your child to eat healthy foods.

❓ Question

Suppose my spouse thinks exerting authority is more important and I believe it's more important to teach her good problem-solving skills. Can we do both?
Differences of opinion about how to rear children is one of the top two reasons for conflict for couples (the other is money). It's very important not to undermine each other in front of children. Find compromises such as you engaging in mutual problem solving with the children and then agreeing to consequences for not sticking to the agreement.

Consider this example. Meredith's mom established a set menu for each day of the week. On Monday morning, it was scrambled eggs and bacon. Meredith hated eggs and had since she was a toddler. But every Monday morning she was forced to ingest a certain portion of the eggs (usually by holding her nose, not chewing, and washing the eggs down with a big gulp of milk). Mom thought Meredith would grow to like eggs or at least tolerate them. There were many other foods Meredith detested as well, and the same scenario played out at the dinner table. Everybody was frustrated with the begging and crying.

After her third-grade year, Meredith begged to go to a two-week summer camp with a friend. Off she went. The camp, unfortunately, served lots of foods Meredith didn't like. The rule for campers was to take one bite of everything before being excused. Breakfasts of toast, two bacon strips and one bite of egg and dinners with about the same amount of food consumption resulted in Meredith losing ten pounds in just two weeks of camp. Meredith survived that week on a sandwich at lunch and a candy bar in the afternoon, which she was allowed to have because she ate the obligatory one bite of everything. Meredith's mom was shocked at how much weight her daughter lost so quickly. What the mother thought was a power struggle was truly about very strong taste preferences.

Meredith was willing to endure two weeks of being hungry instead of eating things she detested. Part of the mother's insistence that Meredith eat things she didn't like is that the mother believed Meredith was being stubborn and that made the mother mad, affecting her ability to use effective problem solving. As a result, the problem went unsolved, with many tears at the table that could have been avoided. So, one important thing you must do when solving your problems or helping a child solve his problems is to be very aware of emotions and how they are influencing behaviors, including yours. If your goal is to assert your authority, force someone to do something, or win the argument, you've compromised your problem-solving ability and your relationships—part of the reason problem solving is a key emotional intelligence skill!

🚨 Alert

It's easy to get embroiled in battles with children and lose perspective about what's most important. That's one reason why it's so important to understand how your emotions are affecting you in any given situation.

Accurately Identifying the Problem

Go back to the case of the balky eater, Meredith. Meredith's mom had decided the problem was about her daughter not eating enough healthy food. But, the reason behind her refusal to eat may need exploration. There could be many contributing factors including too big of a snack after school, snacking too close to dinner time, foods served that she really doesn't like, or that she drinks a full glass of milk as soon as she sits down to eat. And, there could be the defiant explanation that would mean she's not eating well because she gets to eat other things she likes much better if she just waits (remember Wyatt from Chapter 12?).

So, start by asking her why she doesn't eat much of her food at dinnertime. Suppose she says, "I don't like the food." Instead of arguing with her about why she *should* like it, that she needs to eat more healthy foods, or that she ate that food last year, take her word for it. Tastes change. Ask her if there are other reasons. Suppose she says "no." This would be a good time to ask her if she's hungry at dinnertime. Suppose she says "a little bit." Okay, so you've made progress at identifying the problem more accurately and in more detail. She's not very hungry and she doesn't like some of the food. (Notice that you're also doing some reality testing.) Now's a good time to remind her that healthy eating is important and that you want her to help solve the problem.

 **Essential**

Effective problem solving is enhanced by excellent reality testing. Make sure you've gathered all relevant information before you try to help your child solve problems.

Seeking Information

This next step is to find out what foods she does like. That may sound preposterous, but kids have a way of changing their food preferences very rapidly. Go by categories—meats, vegetables (raw and cooked), fruit, and so on. Divide the list into three categories, food she likes a lot, food that's okay, and food she doesn't like.

Another type of information you can explore with her is whether she's eating snacks that you don't know about, for example, when she's playing with her friend next door, and, so on. If you have an after-school sitter come to your home, ask the sitter for information too.

Suppose you find out the following information: which foods she does and doesn't like, that she's not getting extra snacks, but she does come inside a time or two to drink water when she's outside playing. And, she drinks a full glass of milk at the beginning of dinner.

Generating Solutions

Grab a pen and paper and ask your child to think up things that will help her eat more of her dinner every night. Write down all of her ideas for now. Let's suppose she comes up with the following list, probably with some suggestions from you.

- Cook me my own dinner with only stuff I like.
- Let me drink more milk instead of eating some of the stuff on my plate.
- Don't make me eat everything on my plate before I get dessert.
- Let me serve my own food. You give me too much when you serve my plate.
- Let me eat later when I'll be hungrier.

Evaluating Solutions

Here's where the teachable moments occur. Discuss the pros and cons of each solution, which will help build reality-testing skills. This shouldn't take too long, ten minutes at most, or else you may lose her attention. If you have concerns about a solution, explain why. For example, explain that you don't think a second glass of milk is a good idea because she won't get all of the food groups from drinking milk. And, if there's a proposed solution you're just not willing to live with, explain your rationale and remove it from the list of possible solutions. (Tell your child ahead of time that this may happen so it doesn't feel like you've changed the rules.)

For example, you're probably unwilling to cook a separate meal for your child and if you are, explain why.

 **Question**

What if my child cannot think of any solutions or refuses to cooperate?
First, don't get sucked into conflict. Suggest several solutions that you believe represent a win-win possibility and mention those to your child. Ask her whether that option should go on the list of possible ideas. If she refuses to cooperate, that now becomes the problem you must solve first. A lack of cooperation probably indicates the child is very angry. Find out the cause and deal with that issue first.

After you remove options you cannot support, ask the child to pick at least two solutions from the list. Of course, this requires that you have at least two options left, preferably more, so that she does get to choose. Suppose she picks the options of not making her eat everything on her plate before she gets dessert and drinking more milk instead of eating more. Work through ways to implement these options. For example, you could agree that if you serve three things, she only needs to eat all of two of them to get dessert (and then make sure you serve at least two things from her "like a lot" and "like okay" lists). And, you can agree to let her drink more milk but at a slower pace. Get her to agree to a plan where she gets half a glass to begin with and she needs to make that amount last until she's eaten half of her dinner. Then she can have another half glass. After she's eaten three-fourths of her dinner, she can have as much milk as she wants. Get all details of each solution worked out prior to picking one or two to implement. There shouldn't be any surprise details.

Implementing the Solution
Immediate follow-through is critical. Implementing the "eat two things before dessert" and "more milk but at a slower pace"

should begin at the next meal. Gently remind the child about the agreement during the first few meals. You may still get questions like, "Do I have to eat this?" Or, your child may announce she hates broccoli. Remind her that she developed the ideas with you and you chose solutions together. She doesn't have to eat anything on her plate but if she chooses that, she will not get dessert. And, she doesn't have to eat the broccoli as long as she eats the chicken and mashed potatoes.

Don't get into negotiations, change the agreement, or decide too quickly it's not working. Children often increase their efforts to test the limits immediately after new rules or solutions are implemented. They want to test your resoluteness to make certain you really meant what you said about the agreement. So, be patient. Try the new system for at least a week.

Evaluating Solutions

After the solution has been implemented consistently, not half-heartedly, it will be easy to tell if it's working. In the case of the balky eater, she's either eating more and healthier—and with less argument—or not. And, you'll be able to stop cajoling her to eat better foods or not. And, she'll stop complaining about the food choices or not. Success and failure are usually easy to spot.

 **Question**

Is it ever appropriate for a parent just to implement a solution to a problem without consulting the child?
Yes, due to age or for health and safety issues that may need quick decisions, problem-solving alone is sometimes required, but always explain the solution and why you chose it. For most other issues though, a lack of involvement by the child tends to make the solution less likely to succeed because the child isn't invested in the process or doesn't understand the reasons.

Let's assume that for some reason the solutions didn't work. Have a second discussion with your child. Maybe one of the rules needs to get tweaked a bit. Maybe you didn't remember all the different foods the family tends to eat, therefore her "like a lot" and "don't like" lists weren't complete enough. Whatever the possible reasons, it's time to consider other solutions and how they might work if the first ones tried are clearly not working.

Lack of Commitment to the Solution

What if you go through the mutual problem solving process with your child and everything seems to fail, even things the child agreed to do? If failed problem solving is a perpetual problem in your home, you may want to consider offering positive reinforcement for sticking with the solutions and explain consequences that will occur for a lack of follow-through. And, if that fails, it probably means there is a more serious underlying issue that needs to be addressed first.

 Alert

Remind yourself there are always two reasons to engage in mutual problem solving with children. First, they are more likely to abide by the solutions. Second, you are teaching them to understand how their emotions affect them *and* how to apply reasoning to problems. Both skills will serve them very well.

For example, take the case of eleven-year-old Kevin. He played on a year-round soccer team and sometimes there were two or three games per week. He had a bad habit of stripping off his dirty uniform and leaving it in the middle of his bedroom floor or putting it in the hamper inside his closet. His dad had agreed to clean the uniform in time for the next match, but Kevin had also agreed to take it to the laundry room and remind his dad about when his next game was. But, Kevin routinely forgot to take the uniform to the laundry room or tell his dad, instead pleading at the last minute for his dad to clean the uniform. Although having him wear a dirty uniform is a good natural consequence of his actions, that may not bother Kevin, but it could highly frustrate his parents and cause them embarrassment in front of the other parents.

Kevin's parents may want to add an incentive for him to adhere to the guidelines they had developed together. They could reinforce his behavior of getting the uniform to the laundry room the same day he got it dirty by granting him extra TV time or computer time. The reward should be small. If you implement a reward, you could also implement a consequence, helping him understand that if he gets rewarded for doing something, it's also appropriate for him to experience a consequence if he fails to follow through. A consequence of failing to abide by the solution might be that he has to do all of his own laundry that week. Choose a mild consequence first and if that doesn't work, try something a bit stronger.

✅ Fact

Reinforcing desired behavior is always more effective than punishing inappropriate behavior. Try to either implement both simultaneously, or stick with just rewarding appropriate behavior. Punishment, especially when it's more severe, tends to make children angry and resentful.

The Consequences of Poor Problem Solving

You probably know some adults who have experienced challenge after challenge because of their poor problem-solving abilities. Take the case of the dating college students who were enrolled in colleges four hours apart. They had agreed to take turns driving to see each other on weekends, but the boyfriend always had an excuse about why he couldn't drive—a big test on Monday, a home football game—when it was his turn to drive. The female offered up the problem to her psychology class when they were learning the steps of problem solving.

She recognized a problem existed but did not accurately identify the real problem. Her view of the problem was that he was going back on an agreement to drive to see her. That's true, but there was a much bigger issue underlying the unwillingness to drive; in all likelihood—at least his behavior suggested this—he wasn't as committed to the relationship as she was. Recognizing his potential lack of commitment may have increased her anxiety or caused sadness; and, it would require a totally different conversation. If she had been able to recognize how fear and sadness were affecting her reasoning about the problem, she would have solved it much sooner.

What eventually happened? The boyfriend broke up with her at the end of their first year in college and she had spent a whole year driving to another college every weekend rather than having fun with her new friends and going to parties at her school. Almost everyone else could see this developing, except for the young woman. She hid from her emotions, other than anger, but that didn't prevent the unpleasant outcome.

The reason for sharing the above story is quite simple. It's always critical to examine your emotions and how they may be clouding or limiting your thoughts about a problem. Many people believe that problem solving should be logical and analytical and emotions have no place. Yes, problem solving should be logical and analytical—think about the logical process outlined in this chapter—*and* problem solving should take stock of your emotions; otherwise, your emotions may prevent you from being logical.

CHAPTER 14

Impulse Control

How are you supposed to teach young children patience? Or, how to moderate their response to something? Or, how to avoid making a quick decision without really thinking about it? Young children don't have the same emotional and cognitive skills as adults and so they seem impulsive by nature. If a baby is tired of being held, he doesn't patiently wait for you to figure out that his wiggling is a sign of wanting to be put down. Instead, he may just wail loudly or stiffen his body so that you can't possibly cuddle. And, a two-year-old who never throws a tantrum is a rarity indeed.

What Is Impulse Control?

Impulse control is a decision-making skill. If a child does something impulsively, it might be easy to disqualify that as a "decision" because the word impulsive typically includes being swayed by emotions or involuntary reactions. Notice the word emotions? At its core, impulse control is about understanding and controlling emotions long enough to think about a decision before acting. Impulses are never truly involuntary; rather, they seem so because of action taken quickly and without much thought. There are many ways children can act impulsively—giving in to a temptation to eat something or to cheat at a game, acting rashly by doing things such as grabbing a toy from another child's hand, blurting something out while a teacher is talking, spending all of their weekly allowance on the day they get it, or hanging up the phone when angry. The opportunities to be impulsive are numerous.

 **Question**

> **How is spontaneity different from impulse control?**
> Spontaneity means that you have enough flexibility to change plans or a course of action at the last minute or that you engage in a behavior without forethought. That sounds a lot like impulsive behavior. The major differences are in connotation—spontaneity is used to describe actions that are freeing and positive (e.g., spontaneous applause) whereas impulsivity refers to behaviors that are harmful and negative (e.g., impulsive outburst).

Why Impulse Control?

Each impulsive action involves a decision, just not a carefully considered one. Carefully considered decisions tend to lead to better outcomes. Learning impulse control early in life undergirds a child with a skill set that leads to higher school achievement, more relationship success, and better work performance. For example, the child who is a little overweight needs to learn self-control and delay of gratification when related to eating. Otherwise the child will overeat at friends' houses, on visits to grandma, or as a teenager roaming the mall with friends. It's fine for you to help the child control a tendency to overeat, but part of the plan also needs to be teaching the child impulse control.

Marshmallows and Impulse Control

In the early 1970s, psychologist Walter Mischel and colleagues came up with a way to test preschool children's impulse control.

He set up a situation that would tempt most children. The child was asked to take a seat at a table with one marshmallow on a plate right in front of the child. The child was told that the experimenter had to go do an errand and that if she could wait until the experimenter returned to eat the marshmallow, she would get a second one. The experimenter left the room for about fifteen minutes and the temptation began. Would the child succumb to the temptation or would she exercise impulse control? As it turns out, the children, almost one third of them, who exercised the most impulse control not only benefited that day (they got to eat two marshmallows, not one), but their skill in remaining patient and delaying gratification served them well in other areas of life.

Most of the children in the study were the daughters and sons of Stanford University professors and so Mischel and his colleagues were able to locate most of them as high school students in the 1980s. This time the researchers didn't test their impulse control. Rather, they asked for teacher ratings about social effectiveness and popularity with peers, but did not tell the teachers why they were asking for such data or who had exhibited effective impulse control as a four- or five-year-old. They also collected academic data such as SAT scores. What do you think the researchers found?

As juniors and seniors in high school, the high impulse-control children were more likely to have scored, on average, some 200 points higher on their SAT scores, something that was *not* an artifact of different quality of schools or different levels of parental intelligence or education (remember they were children of Stanford professors). And, the researchers found that these high impulse-control children were better liked by peers and experienced better social adjustment.

All of these results happened just because the children didn't eat a marshmallow? No, not exactly. It was their skill in impulse control, something they probably exercised frequently, that likely accounted for the differences. The children who were able to delay gratification as a preschooler probably had better control of their ability to finish their homework before playing. Or, they resisted the urge to listen to another child talking during math class. Or, they remained patient when working on a school project. There are probably thousands of opportunities to give into impulses between ages five and seventeen that would affect how much a child learned. And, it showed in their grades and SAT scores.

 **Essential**

> Watch for signs of poor impulse control as early as the preschool years and intervene immediately, teaching your child how to wait patiently, resist an urge, or think through a decision before acting. These are the foundational skills of impulse control.

But what about popularity and social skills—how did impulse control play a role here? Who would you rather interact with, someone who doesn't interrupt or someone who does? Someone who frequently makes last-minute changes in plans you had with her because something else looked more appealing or a friend who doesn't do this? Would you be likely to get along better with someone who vents anger by yelling at you after the slightest provocation or someone who doesn't get inflamed so easily? Trust and mutuality are key parts of effective relationships, and it's harder to build trust with someone who is unpredictable and tempestuous.

Mischel and his team followed up with many of the original participants when they were in their forties. By then, adult success at relationships and work should be evident. And, guess who was more successful in both arenas? That's right; the child who could delay gratification and manage his frustration was more likely to be successful at work. Think about it. No one wants to work for a boss who makes quick decisions that often backfire, who is likely to send an e-mail blasting people for a small error, or who consistently interrupts you, complaining that it takes you too long to make your point. And, most people don't want to be married to someone like that either!

Impulse control may be one of the more difficult emotional intelligence skills to develop as a teenager or adult if you don't develop it early in life. Why? Because giving into your impulses usually is reinforced in the short term by getting something you want, feeling a release of tension, or some other benefit. Another way to describe this is that impulsive actions are typically rewarded in the short term but not in the long term. And, the more often a behavior is rewarded, even if just in the short term, the more difficult it is to change later.

How Can You Teach Impulse Control?

There are four basic ways to teach impulse control. First, your child will naturally confront situations where he has to exercise some impulse control. You can plan ahead for ways to ensure a greater chance of success. And, when he is successful, praise his actions of waiting or whatever else he did to show restraint. Second, you can create an environment that is more conducive for impulse control, especially if you think your child is struggling to learn this skill. Third, you can point out impulse control when his friends or someone else he knows exhibits impulse control. Talk about how the person exhibited control and what the benefits were. Finally, you can model impulse control yourself.

Confronting Impulses: Spending the Allowance

Suppose you give your seven-year-old $2 a week in allowance money. Most weeks she likes to go to the grocery store with you and buy candy with the money. Because you limit how much candy she can buy, she'll sometimes use a dollar to download a song to her iPod. You know the State Fair is coming to town in two weeks so you suggest she save her money for this week and next week so she can spend it all at the State Fair. You could give her even more incentive to exercise impulse control by offering her an extra dollar for every dollar she saves.

But, the choice is hers. Step back and see what happens. If you go the grocery store, take her along as usual. If she says she doesn't want to go so she won't be tempted, that's great! She's learned that one way to help her control impulses is by removing herself from tempting situations.

Two weeks is a long time for some seven-year-olds to wait so consistently reinforce her behavior throughout the two-week wait. "You made a great decision not to go to the grocery store with me; they had all of the Halloween candy out and it looked very tempting." Or, remind her if the State Fair occurred today, how much extra money she would get from you because she was able to control her spending.

Prior to going to the State Fair, remind her about all of the different booths, games, and food choices. Help her think about how she might want to spend her money once there and what she can do to reduce temptation to buy the first thing she sees. Coach her to ask herself the question, "Will I be happy with myself if I see something later that I like better?" Or, she can ask herself how it will feel to spend her money in the first thirty minutes and then have four hours left with no money to spend. And, teach her how to survey all the possibilities first—going around to different booths and rides—before she chooses where to spend her money.

Making Environmental Changes to Help Create Impulse Control

Suppose your four-year-old daughter is asked to be the flower girl in the wedding of a favorite aunt. She really wants to be in the wedding, but you're concerned about her ability to stand still for that long. She gets very fidgety and thirty minutes is a long time for her to stand without causing some kind of disruption. And, lots of four-year-olds would have trouble standing for this long even if they did have good impulse control.

So, think of environment changes you could make that may help. Instead of her standing for the entire ceremony, she could take a seat beside you in the second row after she walked down the aisle. Or, she could stand at the front for a few minutes, taking a seat beside you at some natural breaking point such as right before or during a song. The latter requires some impulse control but not something that may be too challenging for a fidgety four-year-old. Once seated beside you, have a picture book for her to look at if she gets restless. Your goal is to teach her ways to cope with her impulses that are socially appropriate. Expecting her not to get fidgety is unrealistic. Also, ask her for ideas about what she can do while standing with the other members of the wedding party that would help her stand still. Maybe she wants to hold hands with a favorite aunt who's also in the wedding party.

Think of times you may have made "environmental changes" to help you control your impulses. You've probably chosen not to buy your favorite ice cream at the grocery store or maybe you cut up a credit card; in other words, you found ways to cope with impulses that were within your control. You don't have to tempt yourself by keeping a freezer full of ice cream or carrying five credit cards. Changing the environment to avoid the temptation reflects good coping skills and good decision making!

Alert

Make sure your expectations for behavior are in line with a child's developmental capabilities. For example, a high-energy three-year-old will not sit quietly through most movies in a theater or wait patiently at a fine dining restaurant. Make sure you do your part to prevent putting your child in situations where normal behavior for a child that age would be inappropriate for that setting.

Look around at the environment when searching for solutions to impulse control challenges. Children can sit in different seats at the dinner table if they have trouble keeping their hands off each other. Or, two kids who talk while they're supposed to be doing homework can be given two different spaces to do homework. Or, the child who can't resist taking the pacifier out of his little brother's mouth can be sent to a different room to play (after giving the pacifier to his brother).

A key part of developing impulse control is explaining your reasons for changing the environment. Make sure the child knows that you're deliberately thinking about how to use the environment to help her control impulses. Some families don't allow any TV watching or computer gaming during the week because it's too hard to stop. Temptations are just that—tempting!

Discuss Impulse Control and Why It's Important

You'll find lots of examples of well-developed impulse control and poor impulse control in historical examples, current events, among friends and neighbors, and in children's literature. Pick examples that fit your child's age and interests. A seventh grader who is an avid sports fan may learn about impulse control watching a basketball game with you during which the star player got kicked out of the game for a flagrant foul and the coach got a technical foul. Both situations were caused by poor impulse control. Discuss what happened. Get the child to think about the consequences of the impulsive actions.

As a teenager, the famous tennis player Bjorn Borg had major issues with screaming and throwing his racket when he got upset during tennis matches. Even though he was a rising star, already gaining national attention, his parents made a decision to take his tennis rackets away from him for a few days whenever he lost control during a tennis match. The shorter durations didn't faze him or change his behavior, so they finally took the rackets away for a much longer time.

❓ Question

Should I punish my child if she displays poor impulse control?
Always try to reinforce positive occurrences of behavior, such as rewarding patience and maintaining control, rather than punishing the absence thereof. But, if that doesn't work, use natural and logical consequences (see Chapter 12 for more detail) to help your child learn the costs of impulsive actions.

By the time his parents allowed him to play again, he was desperate to do whatever it took to continue to play. So, as he caught himself ready to scream or throw a racket, he would do something else like mutter under his breath or pace for a few seconds. The more he practiced reacting that way instead of throwing his racket, the better he got. Soon, he didn't even think about having to control his impulse to scream or throw his racket. Those impulses no longer existed. And, Borg went on to become one of the most successful tennis players ever. He earned a reputation for never losing his cool on the court, something that tennis experts believed was a huge advantage because he could maintain his concentration.

Pick examples and famous people to discuss that will interest your child. Explain how the character or person struggled with impulse control and how they overcame it. Talk about the consequences the person suffered when they couldn't contain their rash behavior or avoid a temptation. And, when your child gives in to her impulses, have the same types of conversations.

Model Impulse Control

If you lose control and scream, or overeat, or charge things to a credit card you cannot afford, you're sending your child a mixed message about impulse control. Observe yourself. Does your child hear or see you do things that are rash or an act of giving into a temptation? And, how do you behave when angry? There are calm and effective ways to let someone else know you're angry.

Korrel Kanoy, the author of this book, and some of her colleagues studied various discipline techniques that parents used. They looked at multiple factors that predicted what type of punishments parents used—time out, logical consequences, spanking—how frequently each technique was used and the intensity with which it was delivered. Intensity was measured in minutes (how long did the time out last?), number (how many slaps on the child's bottom?) and/or degree of force (did the spanking leave a red mark?).

Many factors predicted parental discipline styles and frequency. One finding stood out in terms of the frequency and intensity of spankings in particular. Most parents who spanked or used other physical punishment *frequently and with great intensity*—sometimes using harsh methods such as hitting with a belt or pinching on the face—*self-reported that the child had just done something that made the parent very angry.* And, the parents who used these harsher methods with more frequency also *reported feeling less anger after delivering the spanking.* Spanking, delivered with such harshness, sounds like it may be an impulse control issue. If the child angers the parent and hitting the child frequently and forcefully alleviates some of the anger, then the parent is giving in to a temptation to use force because it makes her feel better. If the spanking was being used as a discipline technique and not as an impulsive reaction to anger, the parents in the study talked about how they always took time to calm down and how they typically discussed what the child had done wrong. And, they never mentioned feeling relief from their anger after delivering a spanking. But, the opposite was true with the impulsive spankers.

ⓔ✪ Essential

Always calm yourself down before disciplining a child. Otherwise, you may discipline with too much intensity, causing the child to become fearful of you. The more the child is flooded with fear, the less likely she is to learn the lessons you are trying to teach.

It's best for parents to decide how they want to discipline prior to any child misbehavior. Sooner or later, a child will do something so infuriating that you'll want to lash out with behaviors or words you later regret. Decide now what to do when those situations arise and you'll be better able to manage your own impulses.

Consider this example. Sally's son loved playing with Matchbox cars and was busy at play one day when his mom told him it was time to clean up. She had forgotten to give her son the typical "five-minute warning" which didn't help. When his mom instructed him to clean up right now, Victor threw one of the Matchbox cars at his mom. The car connected with force and immediately caused a big welt to rise. Because Sally had determined she would never physically strike her kids—which she was tempted to do in this situation—she was able to maintain control enough to direct the child to time out.

Sally then left to put ice on the welt while Victor put himself in time out. After taking a few minutes to calm down, she was able to speak calmly with Victor. She showed him the welt on her hand and talked to him about the risks of physically acting out. Victor teared up when he saw his mom's hand and said, "Sorry, Mommy" without having to be asked. By maintaining her impulse control, she was able to teach a far more valuable lesson. In fact, if she had struck Victor, she would have been teaching him that if someone else hurts you, it's okay to hurt them back. And, she would have been modeling poor impulse control.

You've all heard the phrase "actions speak louder than words" and that's certainly true with impulse control. You must model it and actively teach it. Some children will struggle more to gain control over their impulses than others do, but all of them can do so. But, you must lead the way.

Enlist the Help of Others

Other people spend hours of time with your children with you not present, so it's wise to enlist their help with teaching your child impulse control. Otherwise, your efforts to teach impulse control could be rapidly erased.

Grandparents

Most grandparents just want to have fun and enjoy time with their grandchildren. Their days of disciplining misbehavior and saying "no" are behind them. It's going to be challenging for some of them to resurrect these behaviors, especially with grandchildren that they may see only occasionally. Grandparents can be powerful allies so enlist their help!

Enlist their help by explaining the reasons for actively teaching impulse control. Sharing a few of the benefits from the research may help get them motivated to do their best. Keep it simple by giving them just a few guidelines—how to handle a temper outburst, what to do about eating and wanting to overeat, and how to shut down too much TV watching or too much computer time. If they want to give the grandchildren money to spend while they are together, ask them to guide the purchases with an eye toward helping the child think carefully and avoid rash decisions to buy the first thing she sees.

Teachers

Teachers certainly benefit when children display impulse control. In fact, they actively teach behaviors such as waiting your turn, not interrupting, standing patiently in line, and not disrupting other children at work. So, if your child has additional impulse control issues, share them with the teacher and enlist help. In particular, warn the teacher if your child gets easily distracted by other children—a quick fix to such is to change where your child sits to place him beside calmer children. Or, let the teacher know if you're working on not interrupting others or other forms of patience. Or, perhaps your child gets frustrated and impatient with particular types of academic work. Your child could be paired with another child for some "peer teaching" in this type of situation. Given that many teachers manage a classroom of twenty-five or more children, sometimes by themselves, it's always wise to alert a teacher about where your child needs support and what you are doing at home.

 Alert

Don't just assume that others will help teach your child impulse control. It takes fortitude to ignore a temper tantrum or not give in to a crying child. Help others by alerting them to your child's biggest challenges with impulse control and what you do at home to help the child manage his impulses.

And, let the child know that you and her teacher have talked about these issues so she'll know the teacher will be watching for the same behaviors you are. It's always helpful if children know that the expectations and standards between home and school will be consistent.

CHAPTER 15

Flexibility

Flexibility and childhood don't always mix. Parents establish routines, which children need, to help everyone in the family know what to expect and to keep everyone moving in the same direction without constant reminders. So, teaching flexibility may seem counterproductive, but it's not. Flexibility will allow your child to adapt to change without becoming too anxious. Change will occur, whether it's starting school, moving to a new house, or having a best friend move away.

What Is Flexibility?

Flexibility is a skill that enables your child to adapt to changing circumstances or to initiate change. Flexibility allows her to shift priorities easily, say from watching TV to doing her homework. And, flexibility enables her to handle multiple demands or tasks without becoming overwhelmed. Flexibility will enable her to stay calm, no matter how much a situation may change or how much she will be shifting from one task to another. Flexibility is part of the stress management domain for good reason.

Flexibility does *not* mean that your child will be so spontaneous that she'll have no ability to stay focused or will jump around from thing to thing. Also, being flexible doesn't mean that she'll be indecisive. Flexibility instead involves adaptation to your environment.

Fact

Charles Darwin's concept of "survival of the fittest" referred to an organism's ability to adapt to its environment effectively, making it more likely that the organism would survive and live long enough to produce offspring. In essence, he was describing a type of flexibility at the level of species.

Why Flexibility?

Flexibility will equip your child to adjust readily to whatever comes her way. And change will come her way. Think about your parents and the change they've experienced in their lifetimes. Many of them had to learn to work with computers after growing up and working the early part of their careers with typewriters or pen and paper. And they had to adapt to an economy that almost required both of them to work outside the home in order to maintain a desirable standard of living. Some of them adapted to a spouse going off to war in an era long before free long distance phone calls, texting, or Skype.

Essential

Flexible people don't have the need to try to control everything in their environment. Trying to exert control to maintain predictability takes a lot of emotional energy. And, sometimes the effort to control situations rather than adapt to them alienates others.

Here's the point: Change happens whether it's desirable and welcome, or not. Children who know how to adapt to change gracefully will always be less stressed and find more enjoyment in life. They will experience less anxiety when faced with new situations.

As a result, they'll have more physical and emotional energy to use in the situation.

I'm Not Going

Although the following true story involves a college student, it was her childhood experiences that most likely established her inflexibility. Here's the story. Nathalie was a junior in college who was enrolled in a Child Development class. Her professor, along with another faculty member, had planned a summer study trip to Great Britain. Nathalie was a two-sport athlete and excellent student who wanted to earn some academic credits during the summer so the faculty member suggested she join the study-abroad group. Here's how the conversation went.

Professor: I hope you'll go on the summer study trip to Great Britain with us this summer.

Nathalie: No way!

Professor: That seemed pretty definite. Why not?

Nathalie: There's no way I want to go somewhere that I'm not familiar with and have to learn my way around.

Professor: We'll be traveling as a group. And during free time, students always stay in small groups.

Nathalie: Yeah, but I'll be on a totally different sleep schedule and have to eat food I'm not familiar with. I like my routines and I don't want anything to change them.

Professor: Hmm . . . I remember at the beginning of this class you mentioned your reason for taking it was that you want to have children one day.

Nathalie (confused): That's right, but what does that have to do with going on this trip?

Professor: Based on what you've learned so far this semester, do you think you'll have to change any of your routines when you have children?

Nathalie (startled): Oh . . . , yeah, I guess so.

Professor: So, when are you going to start practicing being flexible? The sooner you start, the more flexibility you'll have by the time you have your first child.

Nathalie: Let me think about it.

A few days later the professor asked Nathalie about her decision. Here's that conversation:

Professor: So what about going to Great Britain—have you made up your mind?

Nathalie: I sort of want to, but every time I get ready to tell you I'll go, I get really scared.

Professor: That's expected. Change and new experiences can be scary, especially the more you try to avoid those situations.

Nathalie: You're right. I hate new situations. I had to beg my parents to pay for a single room because I couldn't imagine living with someone else. I like everything in my room put away in a certain place.

Professor (who was also Nathalie's advisor): Nathalie, I think this would be a great way to stretch yourself a little bit and also earn academic credit hours. I'll be one of the trip leaders. The people in the countries we're going to speak English. Yes, some of the food will be different but much of it will be the same. And, you'll get to experience a lot of new things but within the safety of the group.

Nathalie: Okay, I'll go.

As the trip date approached, the professor kept in touch with Nathalie, whose nervousness grew by the day. On the flight over the Atlantic, Nathalie sat by the professor, willing herself not to be too scared (she'd only flown once before). The first few days of the trip, she stuck close to a faculty member. By the end of the first week, she seemed more relaxed and ventured out in the afternoon during free time with a large group of students, something she would have never considered doing earlier in the week.

By the end of the second week, Nathalie had taken on a leadership role within the group, even planning nighttime social outings with small groups of students (and, needless to say, without a faculty member present). In just two short weeks, she had transformed from someone who was scared of anything different and not open to new experiences, to someone who was comfortable finding her way around in a different country. Her confidence grew by the day.

⊕ Alert

Always prepare children for change that is predictable. Preparation will help the child manage her stress better and lead to a more successful experience. That enables her to grow more confident that the next change can be mastered as well.

The last day of the trip, Nathalie connected with her professor for a short conversation. She told her professor what a great experience the trip was, and that she was amazed at how comfortable she had become with new experiences. "I guess I thought change was bad; now I realize it can be terrific!" I'll still probably stick to my routines at home, but now I know that the world won't end if I have to change one of them."

Nathalie was a bright young woman. Her parents had not exposed her to change and the changes she had experienced—such as leaving home for college—were expected and necessary if she was going to be a successful professional. But those changes had always been extremely difficult for her even though they were expected and planned. Now she had a new skill set that would make future changes less difficult.

Routines and Flexibility: Can They Co-Exist?

Having set routines for mealtime, bath time, bedtime, getting ready for school in the morning, saying goodbyes, and a whole host of other things is helpful and even necessary to prevent chaos. Routines give children predictability. They know what is supposed to happen next and what they should do. Routines also keep children focused on the task at hand.

Routines can also be very comforting to children during stressful times. Four-year-old Sam and his mom had a very predictable goodbye routine every morning when she dropped him off at day care. First, he put all his things in his cubby, then he picked out a short book for his mom to read to him, and then she walked him to the "goodbye window," aptly named because kids could watch their parents pulling out of the parking lot from this window. After a hug goodbye, mom left, waved to Sam as she passed the goodbye window on her way to her car. She got in her car, honked the horn twice, and drove off. While that may seem elaborate, it worked for Sam to ease him into his day at childcare.

Question

How can I tell if I'm creating a routine or being inflexible?
Think of routines as established patterns that help you accomplish repetitive tasks more easily, with less thought or need for discussion. Routines help with things that are predictable. Flexibility, on the other hand, allows us to adapt to the unpredictable, unexpected, or unwanted things that come our way.

Bedtime without routines would create chaos in many families. Older children know what is expected and they function independently because of the well-established routine. Trying to get one or more children off to school each morning without established routines would often result in being late, leaving lunch at home, or some other unpleasant consequence for parents or children.

Flexibility and adherence to routines are complementary skill sets, that when combined, enable a child to gracefully proceed through life, neither fighting change nor becoming so rigid that she loses opportunities to grow. A second type of flexibility skill involves being able to initiate a change or lead change. Although this may sound like an adult behavior, it's appropriate for kids to learn how to initiate change. A third type of flexibility involves the ability to shift priorities at a given moment, easily transitioning from one task or activity to the next, without a disrupting impact.

Flexibility as Adaptation

Take inventory of all the change that will be "forced" on your child (in other words, your child will not be able to stop it) before he even gets to be ten years old. Starting a new day care or having a new nanny is something a vast majority of American children experience. Then there's going to school. Whereas some children are lucky enough to have parents drive them to school, most children begin riding a bus, yet another change. Possible changes, ones that many children will experience, include birth of a sibling, moving to a new house, or parental divorce. There's also the possibility that a best friend moves away, a sibling or parent becomes very sick, a grandparent or pet dies, and a whole host of other possibilities.

A child who has gained skill in adapting to the changing circumstances will fare much better in terms of reduced stress, less anxiety, and a greater willingness to explore the opportunities present in the new situation. Resisting change does not stop it, but resistance will make the adaptation much harder.

Preparing Children for Change

Fortunately, most change can be predicted such as starting a new school or moving to a new house. Predictable change gives parents the opportunity to educate the child about what's going to happen. Give your child time—but not too much time—to prepare for the change. But how will you know what's enough time? Three considerations can guide your thinking about timing. First, if anyone is discussing the upcoming change around the child, then discuss it with the child. The timing, in other words, occurs when the child needs to know, such as when they overhear you or an event occurs such as the family making an appointment with a realtor to go look at new homes.

Question

Why is flexibility considered a form of stress management?
The amount of stress a child experiences in a situation depends on how threatened the child feels. If any type of change is almost always viewed as threatening, your child will experience a greater release of cortisol, the stress hormone. Greater stress levels interfere with cognitive function and wear down your child physically.

A second way to gauge timing is to allow enough time to visit the site (new school, hospital) or get comfortable with a new person. This usually involves two or three visits, each lasting a little bit longer. Between visits, do whatever you can to show your child pictures of the place (or new teacher), answer questions, and give additional information. Finally, if there's nothing to show the child and you haven't been talking about the upcoming change, a general guideline is to let the child know one day ahead of time for every year old she is. Going to stay with grandparents in another city while the parents go on vacation should be mentioned only a couple of days ahead of time to a toddler, but a nine- or ten-year-old can be told two weeks ahead of time. Using a calendar to mark off the days before the change occurs will help make it more real for the child.

Another consideration related to change is to anticipate which questions your child may ask and then be willing to answer them simply and honestly. For example, if the parents are going on a cruise while the kids go to their grandparent's home, they may ask if you can call them every day. Whatever the answer, be honest and clear. The more definite the details, the better they will adapt.

Fact

Children below the age of six or seven are very concrete and do not possess a well-developed sense of time. Therefore, use tangible things such as pictures and calendars to help them understand the upcoming change in concrete ways.

Teaching Your Child to Initiate Change

It's bound to happen. You'll lose an opportunity at some point because you did not want to take initiative to introduce change. After all, you've heard the saying, "If it's not broken, don't fix it." There are many things, however, that are not broken but could benefit from change.

Consider this example. Suppose you have a requirement that your kids participate in chores each week. For years, you've assigned which chores each child will do each week. Now, your six-, seven-, and ten-year-old are asking to pick which chores they do. They're getting tired of the same ones over and over, but your fear is that the two younger children won't do a good job at some of the harder chores that you give to your ten-year-old. But, what do you have to lose? Your children are showing initiative! Reward their initiative and their willingness to create change by trying it their way.

Although you may be correct that the seven-year-old will not fold laundry as well as the ten-year-old, is perfectly folded laundry your goal? Remember the concept of social responsibility? The most important lesson of chores is that children must contribute work to the family because they are a member of that group. And, if your seven-year-old can't reach cabinets as high as the ten-year-old but wants to unload the dishwasher, invest in a stepstool! The good news is that each child will probably approach her chores with more motivation (and less argument) because of having a choice. And, you will be teaching them that change, while not always resulting in something that's perfect, certainly has benefits. Adjusting your standards based on the age of the child doing the chore requires a little bit of flexibility on your part, thus you would be modeling flexibility!

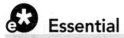 **Essential**

Look for opportunities to have your child initiate some type of change in various areas of his life. Encourage moving around furniture in his bedroom or whatever else comes to mind that could be fun, helpful, or simply a chance to practice initiating change. More practice will bring greater comfort.

Suppose your children never initiate any kind of change. You can teach them how to initiate change. Give each child one of the yearly holidays and ask him to make two or three suggestions about how the family could celebrate the holiday with different or additional traditions. Make sure you set some guidelines or you might end up with multiple suggestions to do expensive things like go to Disney World every year! Then you can have a family meeting to talk about which new traditions to implement and possibly, what things you are currently doing that you want to stop doing. The point is that you're teaching them how to initiate change in a fun way. As you implement some of the suggested changes, you'll be modeling how to embrace new and different things with joy and anticipation, rather than concern.

Flexibility as Shifting Priorities, Activities, or Tasks

It takes flexibility to shift from one task or activity to the next, or to shift priorities, de-emphasizing one thing while emphasizing another. This type of flexibility can be especially challenging for young children who like predictability. Here are some guidelines to help a child of any age, especially a preschool child, shift priorities.

Provide Adequate Notice That a Change Is Coming Up

Alerting a child to change by saying, "You can play for five more minutes before washing your hands for dinner" achieves much better cooperation than "You need to go wash your hands right now." Even adults like warning. You don't want to be told to put down your riveting novel right now to rescue your partner who's knee-deep in painting materials and wants you to pick up a brush. For younger children who don't have a good sense of time, buy a timer and set it to go off when playtime is over. The sand timers are especially effective because young children can watch the sand flow through the hourglass.

Let Your Child Know When She Can Return to Her Activity

When your daughter is really enjoying her playtime, she may prefer to skip dinner and certainly doesn't want to stop to wash her hands. Let her know when she can return to play, whether it's after dinner or the next day when she comes home from day care. This information will help her switch more easily from one task to the other. Still though, you should expect some push back if you're asking your child to leave a preferred activity for a nonpreferred one. Do you like the transition from being off all weekend to going back to work Monday morning? Knowing that she will be able to play again soon will generate more cooperation, but be realistic and don't expect her to be joyful!

❷ Question

What if I don't like the upcoming changes? Should I be honest with my child?
It's preferable to share your honest thoughts and feelings, but do so in a measured way appropriate to the child's age. Suppose a grandparent is moving in with the family, a change no one preferred, maybe even Grandma. It's okay to acknowledge that this is a big change and that some parts of it will be fun and some parts will be hard.

Determine Trouble Spots and Develop Effective Solutions

Four-year-old Maria struggled to settle down each night at bedtime. She was fidgety and asked for additional books to be read to her. Going to sleep sometimes took an hour because she still had so much energy. Her mom came up with the idea of having a longer bath time, giving Maria fifteen minutes to blow bubbles or whatever she wanted to do in the tub. A bath always relaxed Maria so this change in routine helped settle her down a bit. They also started her bath a little earlier than typical. At bedtime, after mom or dad read her two books (a long-standing part of the routine), she was allowed to keep her lamp on and look at books quietly by herself until she got sleepy. All of these changes helped Maria transition from an action-packed day to the calmness needed for sleep.

Instead of Maria begging to stay up later or fidgeting in bed for an hour, she now went to sleep much more quickly.

Some of you may be wondering why changes to Maria's bedtime routine were necessary. Wouldn't it be all right just to set a bedtime and if it took her a long time to drift off, that's okay? The answer to that question depends on your goals. Adjusting the length of her bath and letting her look at books quietly gave Maria the opportunity to try a different approach to bedtime, one that worked better for her. And, her parents modeled flexibility by altering the bath-time and bedtime routines just a bit. Maria still got in bed at the same time but fell asleep more easily, teaching her that it's not the transition itself that is the problem, it's that she needed to approach the transition differently if she wanted to be more successful.

For larger transitions, such as the end of summer vacation to going back to school that fall, prepare your child the way you would for a major change. Begin talking about it, giving the child as much information as possible. For example, discuss what time the child will need to get up, and how his morning routine will change. Remind him where he waits for the school bus so that he can begin to visualize this change in routine.

Be Willing to Answer Questions

Children will ask questions such as "Why do I have to _____?" Answer those questions simply and honestly. And, be willing to answer the "why" question. If you have good reasons for wanting or needing your child to make a transition, sharing those reasons will increase compliance!

What about Unexpected and Possibly Traumatic Change?

Perhaps a tornado ripped through your community, leaving your house in shambles. Or maybe a parent or sibling died unexpectedly.

Maybe the parents decided to separate, something you didn't want to share until you were certain it was going to happen. These transitions are likely to be devastating for adults, too, and sometimes it's hard to attend to children's needs during this time.

Provide extra social support for your child, whether it's by calling a favorite aunt to come into town or by taking off work for a period to be more available. Or, if you need space and time to heal or get business details taken care of, maybe a visit to Grandma's house would work well for your child. Some children will need professional help to cope with unexpected and traumatic changes. Watch for signs of depression (changes in eating or sleep patterns, extreme sadness, drop in academic performance, or listless behavior). And, as soon as possible, return to your typical routines or establish new routines.

The work you've done to help your child be flexible and adapt to change will help in these traumatic situations. In effect, the smaller opportunities served as an inoculation, boosting your child's ability to cope with consequences of the devastating change or event. These changes will be heart wrenching and very difficult, but better flexibility skills will help your child cope.

CHAPTER 16

Stress Tolerance

What happens when your child faces stressful situations? Does he remain internally calm or does he become "tied in knots" and unable to think clearly? Should you set up situations so they produce the least amount stress? Or, is it better to give children practice handling stressful situations? Each child experiences a potentially stressful situation differently depending on his temperament, past experiences, what's at stake, and what he values.

What Is Stress Tolerance?

Stress tolerance describes your child's ability to remain calm in situations she finds stressful. A calm reaction enables her brain to stay focused, whereas a more anxious response interferes with cognitive functioning. Two children can face exactly the same situation, for example, the lead role in a school play, and one may crumble under the pressure and forget lines while the other remains calm enough to remember her lines and perform well. So, it's not the situation that determines the amount of stress your child experiences, it's how she's reacting to the situation that determines her level of stress tolerance. The goal is not to prevent your child from facing stressful situations. In fact, that's impossible, according to the famous stress expert Hans Selye. Why? Because any demand made on your child, even something as simple as getting out of bed in the morning, is a possible stressor at some level. So, the goal is not to prevent stress, but rather you should help her develop skills to become less reactive to stress.

Why Is Stress Tolerance Important?

The ability to withstand stress without being overcome by it will equip your child to face a variety of challenges and still perform well. Less reactivity to stress also means that she'll have lower levels of cortisol racing through her bloodstream. Too much cortisol over too long a period of time takes a heavy physical toll, leaving her more likely to feel tired and more likely to have a lower resistance to illness. Those two outcomes of stress, feeling more tired and getting sick more frequently, only increase the stress experienced. It's harder to focus on homework when tired and missing days of school due to illness creates make-up work. So, an over-reaction to stressful situations can create a vicious cycle that is hard to escape.

 Fact

Even infants can experience stress. A noise that's too loud, being cold for too long, or even being held by someone who's uncomfortable around infants are possible sources of stress. That's why you see infants engage in efforts to self-comfort by sucking on their fist or a finger.

Understanding Stress Reactions

Lots of people misunderstand stress because they believe that situations create stress and that you feel stressed because of the situation. But, that's not correct. Here's why. The amount of stress your child feels is determined by two things: first, how much threat does your child feel in this situation? A second factor involves what resources the child can use to help her cope more effectively. The less threatened she feels and the more resources she has to help her cope, the better she's likely to handle the situation.

Consider this true story. Ashley was a star swimmer on her local summer league team. Many of the other swimmers were members of year-round teams and highly accomplished swimmers who practiced five or six days a week throughout the year, honing their strokes and practicing their flip turns, a key element in a fifty-yard race. Ashley was a talented swimmer who didn't swim year-round and had not yet mastered her flip turn.

When the seedings for the summer league championship meet were released, Ashley was seeded first by .01 of a second. Three talented year-round swimmers were seeded second, third, and fourth, all within .10 of a second of Ashley's time. In essence, all four girls swam equally fast. Adding to the pressure for Ashley was that the fact that her team had a great chance to win the city championship among the twenty-five teams represented, but so did the closest rival team and one their swimmers owned one of the times within just fractions of Ashley's time.

Ashley's coach upped the pressure considerably when he told her he had prescored the meet and her team would win by two points if all the seeded swimmers finished where they were supposed to. That meant Ashley had to win her freestyle race.

The morning of the meet, Ashley was crumbling under the stress. She had a hard time going to sleep the night before and was too nervous to eat breakfast. The meet started at 1 P.M. so she needed to eat to have enough energy. And, the afternoon start meant there was plenty of time to fidget and get nervous in the morning. Her mom tried to help distract Ashley that morning but to no avail. Ashley finally dissolved into tears. Her mom sat down beside Ashley, gently stroked her hair, and said "Mia Hamm is nervous today too." Ashley was a huge soccer fan and the whole family had been excited that the USA women's soccer team had earned their way into the championship game with a chance to win the World Cup. At the mention of Mia Hamm, Ashley blinked back her tears and said, "Really?" Here's how the rest of the conversation went.

Mom: Sure she's nervous. Great players get nervous before big matches because they know how much everyone is counting on them.

Ashley: Like my coach and team are counting on me.

Mom: Yes, they are. But everyone knows you'll try your hardest and do the best you can.

Ashley: But what if I lose?

Mom: Sweetie, finishing in the top five across the whole city isn't losing! But, what would be the worst thing that could happen if the girl from the rival team beats you?

Ashley: Her team could win the championship.

Mom: That's true. And, it's also true that you could win your race and yet your team could finish second in the championship. Or, you could finish second to the girl from the other team and your team could still win the championship. There are 150 other kids on your team and everybody will need to perform well for your team to win. If you give the race your best effort, everyone will support you.

Ashley (tentatively): Do you think the coaches will be mad at me if I don't beat the girl from the other team?

Mom: No, sweetie. No one will be mad. They know how hard you've worked and that you've done your best. And, everyone's excited about how much you have improved this summer.

Ashley (still tentative): Yeah.

Mom: You've worked extra hard in practice this week and even spent two extra hours working with your coach on flip turns.

Ashley: And I've gotten a lot faster.

Mom: You sure have.

Ashley: What do you think Mia Hamm is doing right now? (The soccer match was scheduled to start late in the afternoon.)

Mom: My guess is that she's doing something that she enjoys that will help her relax. Would you like to think about things you could do that would help you relax?

Ashley: Yeah.

They decided that watching one of Ashley's favorite movies would help. So, they started watching together, cuddled up on the sofa. Within twenty minutes, Ashley was sound asleep. She slept for forty-five minutes and woke up hungry. Her mom cooked a breakfast full of carbohydrates and Ashley ate it all. They started the movie again and watched until it was time to leave.

Essential

Understanding your child's temperament and how intensely she may experience a situation will give you cues about how to help her proactively deal with an upcoming stressor. In other words, try not to wait until she's already stressed. Instead, teach her how to be less reactive to potentially stressful situations.

When it was time for the big race, Ashley was nervous but focused. She had done extra practice on flip turns that week with her coach and was feeling more confident about that part of the race. Her stroke was strong and pure and it came naturally to her. She stood behind the block and did what her coach suggested—imagine "nailing" your flip turn.

The gun sounded and the four strong swimmers all started well. Ashley's stroke was the strongest, and she approached the wall at the end of 25 yards with a half-body lead. She flipped. Would she come out of the turn still in first? She did, but with her lead shortened to just a head. She had conquered the hardest part of the race and could see she was leading. She powered her way to the wall, touching just .05 ahead of the second place finisher. Ashley had managed to control her stress reaction enough to perform very well. That outcome did not seem likely when she started off the day short on sleep, not hungry, very fidgety, and crying. Her coach pulled her from the water, gave her a huge hug and sent her off to celebrate with her teammates.

Ashley's mom had reduced both the level of threat by directly addressing Ashley's concern about not winning, reminding her she had 150 teammates who also were swimming that day, and by letting her know that even stars like Mia Hamm get nervous. She gently helped Ashley see that getting upset wouldn't help. And, she equipped Ashley with resources to cope—a fun movie to watch and earlier in the week, supporting her desire for extra practice time with her coach.

Question

What can I do if my child falls apart and is so upset that nothing seems to help?
For younger children, observe what tends to calm them down when they are mildly stressed. Maybe it's holding a favorite stuffed animal or sitting in your lap. Use those resources to help create less reactivity to bigger stressors. For older children, you can create a special spot they can go to when stressed. Make the spot cozy and inviting and let your child control when she enters and exits the area.

Reducing the Threat Level

The first step to managing stress is to minimize the threat. Help your child to ask the question, "What's the worst that can happen in this situation?" More often than not, the worst thing doesn't happen. It's highly unlikely that every kid on the swim team will swim their best race and that the whole championship will come down to one ten-year-old in one race. Ashley's mom helped her to understand that. Another question to ask in a stressful situation is,

"What's likely to happen?" The likely scenarios are usually much less threatening.

Another way to reduce threat is to share examples of a time you faced a major stressor, what was at stake, and how you handled it. Ashley's mom did this using Mia Hamm rather than herself as an example. Being scared to fail or not perform well increases the likelihood of that exact outcome. So, helping the child think less about failure and more about the exciting opportunity is a key strategy to reduce reactivity to stress.

A third way to reduce threat is to get the child to make a list of all the good things that can happen. Suppose your son has to start a new school because you moved to a new house in a different part of the city where the schools are reputed to be stronger. Plus, it's a brand-new school and some of the best teachers in the district have applied to work there. But, your child will need to make new friends in an unfamiliar place. Here's how the list could read of what could go well: a chance to make new friends, new computers in the classroom, a terrific playground, and a shorter bus ride.

🅰 Alert

Children are very tuned in to the important adults in their lives. So, if you're experiencing stress about something, say your child starting a new school, your child will sense your stress no matter how hard you try to hide it. Thus, it's important that you effectively cope with your stress as it relates to situations your child is facing.

Identifying Resources to Help Cope

Resources for coping with stress can include time, help from someone else, a supportive friend or family member, skills, and things that help your child relax. Remember Ashley? Her mom had the time to take Ashley to extra practice sessions and Ashley wanted to spend time that way rather than watching TV or playing with a friend. Another resource they drew on was the coach's skill level to help teach Ashley flip turns. A third resource that helped Ashley was having a supportive mom. Ashley wasn't scared to be herself in front of her mother, and Mom ended up being a valuable resource in this situation. And, Ashley was able to think of something that would help her relax, watching a movie.

Lowering Threat and Using Resources: An Example

Chad and Rosa have been chosen for the lead roles in a classroom play. Chad's temperament is more reserved, and he's a bit shy. Moreover, his parents have very high expectations for his achievement and reward him when he does achieve. They've already promised him they'll buy him a new video game if he memorizes all his lines. His parents are a bit concerned about him being given a lead role in the play, but have not verbally communicated their concerns to him. In fact, they're not mentioning the play very often because they worry that might make him more nervous. The play will be performed before the whole school, something that raises the threat level.

 **Essential**

Helping a child cope with a stressful situation by offering a reward is typically not a good idea. Instead, teach her to think about the stressor differently (reducing the threat) and to use good coping mechanisms. You can always celebrate a successful handling of stress after the fact, but offering rewards ahead of time just communicates to the child how important the situation she's facing is. That will probably increase her stress level.

Rosa, has much the same temperament as Chad. Although her parents also set high expectations, they have been careful not to pressure her. And, they rely on her desire to do well to motivate her rather than providing lots of rewards. They know this is a big chance for Rosa to have fun and to get practice handling a challenging situation. They ask her how she's doing at practice, and she freely tells them when she forgot her lines or said something at the wrong time. Her parents are looking forward to attending the play and watching her perform before the whole school.

The above scenario captures why stress tolerance skills are so important. Chad will undoubtedly experience this situation as more threatening. The more threatened children are by a situation, the more likely they will be to succumb to the stress by becoming internally anxious. The internal anxiety can create cognitive confusion, most likely leading to more errors.

You may believe the deck is stacked against Chad. Yes, his temperament will make him likely to be nervous but Rosa has the same temperament. The way the two sets of parents handled the situation though may have raised the threat level for Chad and lowered it for Rosa. How? First, his parents needed to actively lower the threat. Instead of not talking about the play and promising a reward after it's over, they should have talked with him about the play, lowering the threat through encouragement, stories about times they had to perform, and so forth. They could also remind him of the resources he'll have during the play, such as the teacher standing off to the side who will help if he does forget his lines. And, they could offer to practice with him at home if he wanted to do that. They could help him visualize being on stage and doing well. They could mention how excited they are about coming to the play. Actively coping with the stressor, rather than trying to pretend it didn't exist by refusing to discuss it, creates more opportunities for the child to cope effectively.

Coping Strategies

Have your child identify which coping strategies work well for her and then make sure she uses them consistently and often. Some of these, such as exercise, work well for both short-term and long-term stress relief and others work most effectively closer to the time of the stressful event.

- **Exercise:** Participating in sports, taking a jog with mom, or riding a bike in the neighborhood are all forms of exercise that will reduce cortisol levels. Even doing something simple, like taking a break to do fifty jumping jacks in the middle of a difficult math homework problem, can relieve some stress.
- **Supportive friends or family:** Create the type of environment—using your own empathy skills—in which your child will share concerns or fears with you. This gives you the opportunity to help lower the threat she's feeling or bring additional resources to bear. If you practice the authoritarian style of parenting—high expectations for obedience and achievement and lower warmth—your child may be tentative about sharing her concerns with you. When a child does share her concerns, listen intently and reflect her feelings.
- **Distractions:** Distractions are fine as long as they're not overused. Watching a movie before a big swim meet was relaxing to Ashley. But, if a child watches too many movies, the activity loses its value as a distraction and doesn't help build more active coping skills. Think about a huge project that's due Monday at work. You've got hours of work left to do and promise yourself you'll take Friday night to unwind and then get back to work on the project Saturday morning. But, a friend calls and asks you to play tennis. You agree because you know exercise will help reduce your stress. You return home to find your partner got tickets to the big college basketball game this afternoon. You're still feeling stressed about the project and it will

be good to be distracted a while longer. And so it goes. Distraction may begin to sound a lot like procrastination and when distraction is overused, that can be the case.

- **Positive imagery:** Teach your child to imagine himself in the middle of the stressful event and then doing well. If a big spelling test is coming up and your child gets nervous, help him imagine sitting in his desk and writing down the words just as he practiced them at home. Have him imagine feeling calm and confident. Complete the imagery with him handing in his paper to the teacher with a big smile on his face.

- **Music, reading, or a hobby:** Help your child find a hobby that relaxes her. Maybe she enjoys listening to music on her iPod. Or, maybe she's an avid reader, able to get lost in a book and forget her stressors for a moment. Maybe your child can teach tricks to the family dog. Whatever the case, make sure there is some type of activity she can turn to for relaxation.

Question

What about using relaxation techniques such as mindfulness to reduce stress?
Mindfulness and other relaxation techniques can be very useful as a way to cope with stress and will be covered in Chapter 19. The wonderful thing about relaxation strategies is you can take them with you wherever you go and use them at a moment's notice.

Using the A-E Technique to Reduce Stress

Cognitive psychologists like Albert Ellis claim that rarely do events or situations cause emotional responses, and thus the amount of stress experienced. Instead, Ellis contends it's your interpretation (beliefs) about the event and how it might threaten you or what it may mean for you that is crucial to your level of stress.

Suppose your fifth-grade daughter is taking a standardized test to determine whether she'll get into an academic program for gifted children. She tells herself that you'll be really disappointed if she doesn't do well, even if you've made every effort to avoid putting any pressure on her. Her belief that her parents will be disappointed in her causes her to feel more nervous. And, instead of talking about the situation with her parents as she normally would, she doesn't want them to know how scared she is. So, because of her belief, she's more nervous then she would be normally and is not talking with her parents as she typically would. Another student facing the same standardized test doesn't think that her parents will be mad. She's remembering what they always say, "Just do the best you can, that's all we ask."

 Fact

One of the consequences of stress is that you tend to experience cognitive disorganization. It's harder to remember things, stay focused on a task, or organize your thoughts. Those experiences then increase the amount of stress experienced.

Who do you think will perform better on the test? It's likely the first student will perform worse on the test because her anxiety is so high that it will interfere with effective performance. Both students faced the same event (action), but their beliefs created different emotional reactions and behaviors. To stop this tendency, children need to learn positive self-talk. And, if they go down a negative path, they need to recognize that and challenge their negative thoughts. Here's each step of the A-E model.

- **A= Action:** Some event has occurred or is about to occur (e.g., the standardized test).

- **B= Beliefs:** Rational beliefs involve positive self-talk such as "I can do well." Irrational beliefs, which involve negative self-talk (e.g., "I don't do well on tests"), lead to more emotional distress.

- **C= Consequence:** Irrational beliefs lead you to engage in behaviors that are premature, unjustified, or otherwise off base or not wise (e.g., not talking with her parents about her fear of not doing well). Irrational beliefs are also likely to cause fear, anxiety, anger, and other negative emotions.

- **D= Dispute:** The best way to get rid of irrational beliefs is to dispute them with facts and evidence from past experiences. In this case, your daughter might remind herself about how well she's done on tests in the past. Or, she may remember the time she did receive a poor score and you were very understanding and helped her bring the score up.

- **E= (new) Effect:** Once your daughter has challenged the irrational belief, it is easier to experience a calmer reaction, which should also boost her performance.

You don't need to take her through all the steps of the A-E process each time she's in a potentially stressful situation. But if you sense she's not handling a situation well or engaging in negative self-talk, ask her what she's thinking about the big test. If her response comes back something like, "I'm scared of messing up," then you know you need to help her reframe the situation so she can stay calmer. Teach her positive self-talk messages to use in a variety of situations and that will become another resource she can draw on in stressful situations.

CHAPTER 17

Optimism

The benefits of optimism to both physical health and emotional health have been well publicized since Martin Seligman published his famous book in 1990 titled *Learned Optimism: How to Change Your Mind and Your Life.* So what is it about optimism that makes it so powerful? Like stress tolerance and happiness (which you learned about in Chapter 16), optimism, or rather its opposite, pessimism, has been associated with changes in brain chemistry that occur during depression. Optimism involves far more than just expecting good things to happen. In fact, that oversimplification can be very misleading because optimists help to make good things happen by their positive perseverance.

What Is Optimism?

Optimism, simply described, involves the skill of framing an issue or event in a positive way as opposed to a negative way. But, it's more than that. Optimism has a second part, perseverance, that helps children remain determined and focused when they encounter challenges. Together, they make a powerful combination—a positively framed belief that is supported by the willingness to persist, even in the face of adversity.

So, the child who believes he will score lots of goals in soccer but is never willing to practice and hasn't scored in a game yet, is probably struggling with poor reality testing rather than possessing optimism. But, that same child would be demonstrating optimism if he said something like this, "I want to get better at soccer. I know I could score some goals if I just practice hard enough and listen to what the coach says." And, if the child is still practicing hard after three weeks even if he has yet to score a goal, he would be demonstrating the persistence part of optimism. The classic children's book *The Little Engine That Could* incorporates both parts of optimism.

🔔 Alert

Remind yourself throughout this chapter that a child's level of optimism is *not* determined by the situation. Rather, the level of optimism is determined by how she chooses to frame situations.

Here are some things optimism does *not* mean. First, it's not disconnected from reality. If a student expects to earn an A but has a C average before the last test, this is not optimism. Nor does optimism involve cockiness such as, "I'm so good at dancing I know I'm going to be picked for the 'Dancer of the Year Award.'" Finally, optimism does not happen only in easy or simple situations. The true optimist can call on optimism in any situation. Optimism involves how a situation or issue is framed, regardless of how difficult the situation is.

Why Optimism?

A classic study in psychology demonstrates what can happen when optimism is lost. Dogs were constrained by harnesses in an area where the floor was lined with electrical shock panels. The dogs in the first group could stop the shock by pressing a panel with their noses and quickly learned how to stop the shock. The second group of dogs, however, could do nothing to escape the shock. At first, the dogs in the second group barked, clawed, jumped and did everything else possible to escape the container.

A little later the same dogs were put in a shuttle box with no harnesses. The dogs faced a low wall that could easily be jumped over. As the shock was delivered, dogs in the first group quickly jumped over the low wall. Dogs in the second group, however, did not attempt escape even though they were not harnessed and the way out was obvious. Why didn't they try to escape? Seligman, the lead researcher, and his colleagues termed the dogs' behavior "learned helplessness," an apt but sad term. The dogs had given up (failed to persist) in solving the problem of how to escape the shock. Here's the most important point of all: It wasn't the situation that prevented escape the second time for the dog (there was an escape route); rather, it was the dog's choice. The loss of hope and helplessness crippled the dog, preventing constructive responses to the situation. Optimism is important because it gives hope and fuels the drive to persist through challenges, adversity, or even boredom.

 Fact

Learned helplessness is one reason some students experience academic difficulty. For example, if your son struggles to work math problems with little success, he may begin to give up and not even try to work problems that are assigned for homework.

Pessimism, Learned Helplessness, and Depression

There's a price to pay if someone engages in too much learned helplessness or "I can't do this." That belief is often accompanied by a lack of effort to solve problems. Without persistence to solve problems—the perseverance part of optimism—the problem typically does not get solved or go away on its own. The problem or problems create more adversity, which can lead to more pessimism, and eventually learned helplessness or depression is likely. The strong correlation between learned helplessness and depression serves as a clear warning—teaching optimism is critical to children's overall development. If driven by pessimism, which may eventually lead to learned helplessness, worse and worse outcomes will follow. Unfavorable outcomes lead to a lack of effort, which then almost ensures more negative outcomes. It's a vicious cycle. But, you can prevent your child from getting stuck in this cycle by teaching optimism. Remember, Seligman's book is titled *Learned Optimism.*

 **Essential**

Pessimism will not change facts or circumstances, but it will make dealing with them far more difficult and even more emotionally painful. And, it can reduce the chances of success.

If you want your child to learn optimism, you must model it. Children watch and listen; they do what you do. So, step one is to monitor yourself and change your approach from a pessimistic one to an optimistic one if needed. Second, you need to teach your child about framing situations positively and give her plenty of practice. This step is similar to a coach sending players through multiple drills and exercises, knowing that the more something is practiced, the more it becomes automatic, even in the middle of a pressure-packed game or match. The third component involves reacting with optimism, even in the midst of the most difficult circumstances.

Modeling Optimism

Start listening to yourself as you face various situations or hear news. Your own tendency to be optimistic or pessimistic will be obvious in your words. Most everyone has heard the analogy about the "glass half full" or "glass half empty" way to uncover someone's optimistic or pessimistic tendencies. Begin listening to your way of framing things.

Suppose you had a medical condition and the doctor told you to drink 64 ounces of water a day. You're the type of person who has never drunk much water, maybe a glass a day, and drinking 64 ounces will be a huge change. To help you measure your water intake, you've bought a 32-ounce bottle. At 4 P.M., the first bottle is empty, leaving you with another 32 ounces to drink for the day. The optimist focuses on the positive—"I've already drunk half my quota for the day. I'm taking in lots of fluids which will help my health." Framing the event positively energizes you to keeping drinking and focus on the goal of 64 ounces. The pessimist, in contrast, frames the situation negatively—"I'm only halfway through my daily quota. I'll never get up to 64 ounces. It's hard to drink this much in one day."

ⓔ❗ Alert

Listen to yourself. Are you often negative about things, focusing only on the bad outcomes or predicting doom and gloom? Do you think a lot more about what could go wrong than what could go right? If so, you are modeling pessimism.

The facts don't differ—you've drunk 32 ounces and you have 32 ounces left to drink. The other fact is that the doctor told you to drink 64 ounces a day to improve your health. Some people erroneously believe that the facts in a given situation force them to be negative. Granted, the facts in some situations are horrific. Still, the person who can find some way to stay positive and tackle the situation (perseverance or persistence) will almost always fare better.

Are You an Optimist?

Do this exercise to help you determine whether you are more naturally an optimist or pessimist. Imagine that you are the ninth child born to a family that has twelve children. Both parents work outside the home and the family is able to live comfortably and pay the bills, but doesn't have much money left over for the newest clothing styles, vacations, or new cars. Children are expected to get a part-time job when they're sixteen.

Now, make a list of all the good or bad (pleasant/unpleasant; positive/negative) things about being in this family. After you've completed your list, separate it into two groups: good (pleasant, positive) statements and those that refer to something bad, unpleasant, or negative. For example, if you said that you would always have a large selection of clothes to pick from, even though they are mostly "hand-me-downs," that would be positive framing. If, on the other hand, you said you probably wouldn't get to pick out new clothes for yourself very often, you'd be framing the situation negatively. Both statements or ways of framing the situation are accurate and likely to occur. One's not more accurate than the other, but one is definitely more optimistic than the other. And, if you are the ninth child and you've outgrown your current pair of tennis shoes, would you rather be the optimist who is looking forward to sorting through the available tennis shoes to find the ones you like the best or the pessimist who feels sorry for herself because she can't buy a new pair? The optimist is "making lemonade out of lemons" while the pessimist is sucking on the proverbial lemon when thirsty.

Optimism and Self-Talk

Optimism (and pessimism) often results in self-talk, or things you say to yourself but may not speak out loud. Here are some phrases you may think (self-talk) or even say out loud if you're an optimist:

- Here's a way we can make things work.
- There's always another option that can be considered.
- How can I make this a win-win situation for everyone involved?
- What else can I do to make things better?
- I'm encouraged by your progress.
- I can get better at this.
- I am getting better at this.
- I've made enough progress to tell things will continue to get better.
- The only way I'm going to make this problem go away is if I keep trying.

 **Essential**

Being optimistic does not guarantee that you'll conquer every disease, make every problem disappear, or even that you'll lead an easier life. What it does ensure is that when you face whatever comes your way, you'll do it with positive energy and a desire to "attack" the problem rather than spewing negative energy or helplessly sitting by while the problem engulfs you.

Now, consider a pessimistic alternative to each of the above.

- I don't see how we can make things work.
- We've tried everything and nothing has worked. I'm tired of trying.
- There's no way we'll resolve this conflict in a way that makes everyone happy.
- There's nothing left to try. It is what it is.
- The progress you've made is not good enough.
- I'm not good at doing this.

- I'm not getting any better or making progress.
- The pace of progress has been too slow.
- I can't make this problem go away so I should quit wasting energy on it.

Practicing Optimism Using Positive Framing

Simply put, optimism involves framing situations to find the good, the possible, or the hope. Framing is about self-talk. What does your child say to herself about the upcoming dance recital? Is she more likely to say "It'll be so much fun to perform in front of people?" Or, does she say, "I'll be so nervous in front of all those people that I probably won't do well." Which child do you think will perform better given the self-talk of each? The second child is making a mistake-prone performance more likely by what's she telling herself, a form of the self-fulfilling prophecy.

The Self-Fulfilling Prophecy

The self-fulfilling prophecy states that people will perform up to or down to the expectations others have for them or that they have for themselves. There's plenty of research to support just this phenomena. The self-fulfilling prophecy works like this. A teacher (much of the research has been conducted in educational settings) expects a child who has low standardized tests scores to not perform well (a negative framing of the facts). Thus, he—sometimes unwittingly—pays less attention to that child and provides less help when the child gets stuck on something. Not surprisingly, the child doesn't perform well. The teacher had negatively framed the situation—this child won't do well or cannot learn much because of low scores—and then engaged in behavior that, unwittingly, ensured the child did not succeed. If others' expectations can be that powerful for your child, what about his own expectations and ways of framing situations? And, what will happen to a child's positive expectations and framing if important adults don't support that framing?

Listen to how your child frames a situation. When you hear positive framing or witness perseverance, point it out. Talk about the value of staying positive and persevering. And, when you hear negative framing, stop your child and have a discussion with him. Ask him, "What's another way you could look at this situation?"

Question

How would very strong skills in reality testing affect optimism?
Reality testing, or scanning the environment for information and reacting to the information appropriately, may seem to conflict with optimism. But, the two don't conflict. Reality testing allows your child to gather and understand facts, while optimism reflects how your child frames those facts and how willing she is to overcome whatever faces her.

Still Learning

Suppose your child comes home from school one day and says, "I can't draw and the teacher put up all of our drawings. I know the other kids will make fun of me." The negative characterization of his own skill—can't draw—implies he's already given up trying to do better. Tell him the story (research study) about the dogs that refused to try to escape from the shock even though they could. Or, tell him a story of when you tried really hard to get better at something and you did get better. Offer to sit down and draw with him and make it a fun activity. Let him know he will get better the more he practices.

But what about part two of his sentence? He's expecting something bad to happen; he believes he will be teased. His negative framing will probably increase the chance of being teased because children have a keen eye for who will be bothered by teasing.

So, his framing (belief) that he will be made fun of has a greater chance of happening because of what he's telling himself! Since you cannot be sure whether the other kids will tease him or not, and believing they will may actually increase the chances of teasing because it creates a self-fulfilling prophecy, help him focus his mental energy elsewhere.

Help him focus on staying positive and persevering. Remind him that practice will help him get better and ask him, "What could you do if they do tease you?" Help him generate a list of positive statements he can verbalize out loud or just repeat to himself such as, "I'm practicing my drawing so I can get better." Or, "I like my picture because . . . ," or "The teacher will post our poems next week and I'm really good at writing poems." And, if you think it's necessary, have him practice being assertive to other kids who go too far with their comments (see Chapter 8).

Helping your child frame the situation differently will help take some of the sting out of the teasing if it does occur. And, he'll learn that if he frames things positively, he'll feel better and be more ready to face whatever comes his way.

Mustering Optimism: Justin's Life

Practicing how to be positive and persistent with smaller events will give your child the skills she needs to face the most challenging situations in her life. Consider this true story. Justin was diagnosed with a deadly cancer at age seven. His parents made a decision to only share facts with him—not speculations or guesses—and that when they did share facts, they would also frame things in terms of what they could do to fight the disease (optimism). They never promised he wouldn't die of the disease, just that they would fight it hard (persist), stay hopeful, be positive, and direct their energy to fighting the disease.

ⓔ❓ Question

Is it better to just not share traumatic information with children or to share it and try to be optimistic?
If the traumatic information will somehow affect their lives or they will eventually find out, share the information and how you plan to persist and remain positive. Children can tell when something is wrong and not communicating with them can make it harder for the child to adjust.

Justin, a very intelligent kid, knew that his prognosis was not good, yet he remained optimistic through the many days spent in the hospital receiving chemotherapy or recovering from surgeries. It would have been easy for Justin or his parents to quickly sink into what his mother called a "pity party." Yes, they were all very saddened by Justin's disease and angry about him getting stricken with cancer. Those were their emotional reactions and they were real. Emotional reactions are different from optimism, which determines how someone chooses to react behaviorally. Being very sad or angry about a cancer diagnosis does not mean you or your child has to quit living or believe that bad outcomes are just around the corner.

Focus on Cures, Not the Disease

How did they demonstrate optimism during such a painful time? His parents realized that framing his illness negatively would not help him or them to cope better. A pessimistic framing would sound something like, "He's going to die of this horrible disease and there's nothing we can do to stop it. They don't have very good medicines yet." Optimistic framing, which the family did, sounds like this. "Justin has a horrible disease, but we're going to do everything we can to fight it. Researchers are coming out with new drugs every year. Maybe they'll find one that eradicates his cancer. We need to stay one step ahead of the disease and always know what treatment strategy we can use next if the current one doesn't work."

Think about their framing—they acknowledged the ravages of the disease and that there wasn't a cure yet, but also remained hopeful (positive) a cure would be found if they kept trying new drugs and approaches (persistence). In fact, over the six years that Justin lived after his diagnosis, there were new medicines available.

A "Normal" Life

As a result of the parental framing, Justin also had a positive outlook. He maintained normal activities such as playing baseball and basketball. In middle school, he participated in school dances, sometimes with a bald head covered with a baseball cap or stocking hat. Instead of fearing others' reactions to his bald head, he didn't let it stop him from doing fun things. And, other kids in the class followed his lead. Teachers at his school even suspended the "no hats in class rule"; Justin's determination to go to school throughout chemotherapy—which drained him—energized everyone and gave him a much-needed boost—interaction with peers and a respite from thinking about his cancer.

Alert

Some people claim that pessimism is preferable because they are never disappointed with bad outcomes. But, that framing also means they spend a lot of their lives waiting for or expecting bad things. Is that what you want for your child?

Perseverance

Just six months before he died at age thirteen, Justin delivered a moving speech to a group of doctors and researchers who had gathered for an annual conference to learn more about his form of cancer and share knowledge and treatment strategies. Justin acknowledged the seriousness of his disease (a fact), but then went on to talk about all of the progress doctors and researchers had made since the time of his diagnosis (also a fact). He inspired everyone to keep working hard to find a cure (optimism).

About ten days before his death, no longer able to speak or sit up by himself due to a loss of muscle control, Justin continued to show optimism, both the positive and persevering parts. He had just returned from physical therapy (PT) that was ordered to try to maintain his muscle strength. This particular PT session had been very hard, with Justin struggling to perform simple exercises. He was beyond exhausted at the end of the session. His hearing was fine though and he heard the physical therapists encourage his parents to have him sit up in a chair as much as possible so that he would not lose more muscle tone.

They wheeled Justin back to his room and were about to lift him into his bed when he pointed to the chair. So, they placed him in the chair instead. He then pointed to a white board and marker, his only form of communication other than gestures, and began to scribble out a word. He wrote a single word on that white board: "perseverance."

Justin's profound optimism did not prevent his death. But, it did make those six years more hopeful and certainly more bearable; hope fueled his energy to go to dances, hang out with friends, play sports, and not sink into depression about his fate in life. If he had chosen the pessimistic route, he would have been much more likely to give up, ultimately leading to a life spent waiting to die. He could not change the facts of his disease, but the choices he and his parents made to find hope where they could and stay positive made the quality of his life and their life together for those six years more joyful and fun. If you'd like to read more about Justin's inspiring story, go to *www.chordomafoundation.org* and search by the name "Justin Straus" or "Perseverance Pledge."

CHAPTER 18

Happiness

Happiness is the internal joy that relates to satisfaction with who you are (self-regard), the quality of your relationships (interpersonal relationship), what you're doing and how much you enjoy it (self-actualization), and how you're choosing to frame what happens to you (optimism). Another way to explain happiness is to think about a pyramid with the top block signifying happiness. It's the blocks below and the stability of each that will determine how high that pyramid can be built and what events it can withstand.

What Is Happiness?

Happiness is an internal sense of satisfaction or joy. Happy people approach life with more energy, are more cheerful, and display more enthusiasm and energy for new endeavors. Think about what a happy dog looks like. She'll wag her tail a lot, greet you at the door with yelps of delight, eagerly anticipate the next walk, and jump into the car with excitement when it's time for a family outing. The dog lives life fully, with enthusiasm and joy for what's happening now and what will happen in the future. And, everyone loves a happy dog, ensuring that the dog gets more and more positive attention.

Most positive external events have very little if any, long-term benefit in boosting happiness. You and your child may find great short-term joy in her being the best player on the basketball team or the smartest student in class, but those things are not enough to sustain happiness over the long term. In fact, those situations aren't likely to produce much joy except for in-the-moment experiences such as when she shows you her report card or while you're watching her play a game. But these events are transitory and cannot sustain happiness.

✪ Essential

Happiness must come from within. Teach your child to rely on herself to create her happiness and not to expect others to create happiness for her or give her things that will produce happiness.

The four emotional intelligence skills mentioned above—self-regard, self-actualization, interpersonal relationship, and optimism—will predict your child's happiness. The fastest way to improve happiness levels is to develop each of these characteristics. Even if just one of those EI skills is low, it could significantly lower your child's happiness level.

For example, the child who has goals and meets them (self-actualization), has good friends and good family relationships (interpersonal relationships), and who is positive and persistent (optimism) possesses three of the four EI skills associated with happiness. But, if she's not accepting of herself and not confident because of poor self-acceptance and high self-criticism, her happiness level will be impacted significantly.

The child who doesn't participate in meaningful activities that provide satisfaction and a challenge, allowing her to set and accomplish goals, will not be as likely to be as happy as a child who does possess these characteristics. Or, suppose your child liked and accepted herself, participated in activities that challenged her and gave life meaning, and approached things with a positive spirit. But, if she does not have close friendships or strong connections within her family, her life will be void of meaning that comes from a relationship that is mutual and rewarding. Finally, if your child had self-regard, self-actualization, and strong interpersonal relationships, but tended to frame most things negatively, she would spend time each day anticipating doom and gloom, an obvious drag on happiness.

 Fact

The emotional intelligence wheel shown in Chapter 1 puts well-being and happiness all around the wheel because all elements of emotional intelligence work together to produce overall well-being.

Contrary to popular belief, there are very few demographic or life circumstance factors that guarantee (on the one hand) or prevent (on the other hand) happiness. Psychologists have studied age, race, ethnicity, sex, amount of money earned, and many other factors. Other than poverty, which is associated with lower levels of happiness, and very old age, when the elderly become more vulnerable to depression, demographic characteristics matter very little.

Why Happiness?

Happiness is one of the few emotional intelligence skills that has the potential, if underdeveloped, to throw your child's life awry. If the unhappiness is allowed to grow, and it typically does if changes are not made, the risk becomes greater and greater that your child may end up experiencing a mild or possibly severe form of depression. Even mild depression casts a gray cloud over most activities, resulting in a child going through the motions of life but without much joy. And, clinical depression, if the unhappiness grows to this level, is debilitating, affecting all aspects of life.

Does Temperament Influence Happiness?

Studies of temperament differences in newborn infants show distinct patterns—physically active or not, emotionally reactive or not—that have to be the result of inheritance or conditions in the prenatal environment. Children's temperaments have been classified on continuums that range from difficult to easy, active to passive, emotionally reactive versus not reactive, and so on. The point is that your child is born with certain temperamental characteristics, ones they inherited from biological parents, so don't hold the child accountable! But temperament only accounts for about 50 percent of the variance in child behaviors, so the remaining 50 percent can be the result of environmental impact, which includes parenting styles. Your job is to react appropriately to the temperament; because doing so will allow for the greatest development of happiness. For example, an emotionally reactive child may require more patience on your part; if you can't muster this patience, the result could be that you inadvertently harm the child's self-regard because it's difficult for you to be accepting of who she is. Therefore, she may experience difficulties with self-regard, ultimately affecting her happiness.

Shyness

Shy children excrete more cortisol (the stress hormone) in unfamiliar settings or when part of a large crowd. Their physiological reaction to such situations is palpable. Thrusting them into those situations without support or coaching from you will probably lead to more anxiety the next time. Anxiety and depression commonly occur together, so help your child get control of his anxiety as young as possible.

Fact

Children who are shy and anxious tend to have more difficulty establishing friendships. But without supportive friendships, their shyness and anxiety can worsen, making it even harder to gain happiness from a very important source of happiness for children: friends.

So what can or should the parent do in those situations? Step one is to prepare the child. If it's a major transition, take your child on multiple visits to the place such as a new school. If it's a smaller transition such as a new babysitter, have her come thirty minutes before you need to leave to allow for a "get-acquainted" time. Answer questions about the new situation honestly. Provide extra support until the child gets used to the new place or person. Allowing a shy child time to adjust will boost his self-regard (it's okay to be shy; I don't have to dislike myself because of it) and interpersonal relationships will develop faster because your child will be more comfortable.

 **Question**

What is the difference between shyness and introversion?
Introversion is a personality characteristic that indicates your child gets her energy from within herself; thus, alone time to read or do another solitary activity recharges her batteries. She also thinks through things carefully before speaking and enjoys focusing on one activity at a time. Introverts aren't necessarily shy. Shyness creates a strong physiological reaction when children are placed in new situations where they may be expected to interact with new people.

Passivity

Some children are naturally fairly passive. The risk for this child is that he may not command enough attention and is easy to leave in a playpen, in front of the TV, or quietly reading to himself. The happiness challenge with this type of temperament is that the child's opportunities to connect with others—friends and family— may go down significantly. Parents of active children (and active does not mean ADHD) work much harder to keep the child entertained, whether by playing with her more, going on family outings, inviting friends over, or encouraging the child to play outside with other children on the street. Each interaction and each new thing your child tries can boost her self-regard and interpersonal relationship skills. And, one of these family outings may lead her to discover a passion that she begins to pursue, enhancing her self-actualization. She's getting more attention from you, interacting more with friends (interpersonal relationships) and experiencing different things that are likely to build confidence. Passive children, on the other hand, don't demand much. It's up to the parents to carve out plenty of playtime, family outings, and play with friends even though the child doesn't seem to need it.

Emotionally Reactive

Emotionally reactive children are the ones who get upset easily. They also experience joy more intensely. As infants, they may have cried more often or for longer periods of time than less reactive children. These children may react more intensely to situations or changes in their environment or routines and that's their normal pattern. Monitor their reactivity to make sure they are expressing a full array of both positive (happiness, excitement) and negative (distress, sadness) emotions. And make sure to manage any frustration you may have about the child's reactivity or else you will create more reactivity!

What Role Do Events Have in Creating Unhappiness?

External events can definitely contribute to unhappiness because they often are affecting one of the four areas of emotional intelligence that undergird happiness. For example, marital separation may mean your child doesn't see his dad as often, thus affecting interpersonal relationship functioning and maybe even self-regard if he partially blames himself for the separation, something younger children do sometimes. Maybe a favorite grandparent died (interpersonal relationship). Or maybe something's happening at school to erode self-regard such as a hyper-critical teacher.

Alert

Typically, it's not an event that causes unhappiness but how the family and child handle the event. For example, children from divorced families sometimes report that they have more interaction with their fathers, are relieved not to be exposed to conflict, and so on. But, parental divorce, if not handled well (e.g., parents bickering in front of children or putting children in the middle of a conflict), can create lots of distress.

Consider this true story of temporary unhappiness. Shondra was a happy third grader who had lots of friends and did well in school. But, she had become more subdued at home and clingy at bedtime, wanting her mother to lie down with her. The mom knew something was wrong but had no idea what it might be. So, she decided to adhere to her daughter's request to snuggle with her at bedtime (the mom showed empathy by understanding that whatever it was bothering Shondra was probably a huge deal to her daughter). On the third night, Shondra started crying. Mom convinced her daughter that it would be safe to tell her, no matter what was going on. To the mother's horror, she learned that a little

boy in her daughter's class had been sending her sexually sugges-
tive notes and hanging around her very closely on the playground.
The daughter was scared but also embarrassed. The next day the
counselor called in the boy's family and showed them one of the
notes. He was disciplined and immediately transferred to another
classroom. Shondra returned to her normal happiness levels after
a few days. The lesson is simple: If your child quickly transforms
from happy to unhappy, find out what has changed and deal with
it quickly.

Parenting Behaviors and Happiness

Be sure your ways of interacting with your child support the development of happiness. Do a check of how your behaviors either
build or detract from her self-regard, self-actualization, interpersonal relationships, and optimism.

Parenting, Self-Regard, and Happiness

Do you allow your child to have weaknesses? Or, do you push
for perfection in most everything? Everyone has weaknesses, so
modeling your own self-acceptance, despite your weaknesses,
communicates to your child it's okay not to be perfect. It's going to
be hard for most kids to have high self-regard if the parent is consistently critical, pointing out what's wrong, how the child didn't
measure up, or what needs to be improved.

Another way to harm self-regard is to hover too closely, staying on top of your child about what she should be doing, how she
should be doing it, and so on. If you do that, you're sending a sub-
tle message that you don't trust your child's judgment about even
the simple things. That will erode her confidence. Give your child
some room to make mistakes and then let her learn from them.
For example, rushing through her math homework may result in a
careless error or two. If you let her experience the consequences

of that (a lower grade), she'll learn a lot more than if you hover over her, making sure she carefully proofreads her work.

✅ Fact

The authoritarian parenting style is the style most frequently associated with children's anxiety. The uninvolved parenting style may be an artifact of parental depression, leaving children to fend for themselves. Children with depressed parents have a higher chance of becoming depressed themselves.

If you want to build healthy self-regard, make your feedback descriptive, not evaluative. "You spent an hour working on that science project and stuck with it even when you got frustrated" is better than "You did a great job working on your science project today." Why is descriptive language better? First, the child will know what specific thing she did that is worth repeating. And, kids quickly figure out if something can be great, it can also be horrible; evaluative language cues your child into the fact that you are constantly evaluating rather than supporting. So, both positive feedback and constructive criticism should be delivered based on specific behaviors that are worth repeating or should be avoided.

Parenting, Self-Actualization, and Happiness

Simply put, children are happiest when they are achieving goals they've set for themselves and involved in activities that are meaningful to them. Remember the story of the seven-year-old who was a nonswimmer but who really wanted to be on the summer swim team? He found his own niche and achieved great success. Would he have been likely to earn an athletic scholarship to college if his parents had picked out a sport for him and then forced him to do it?

Remember also that achieving goals or doing well at something —even in the absence of a stated goal—is very satisfying. Children need you to support them to do well, not try to make them do well with threats or excessive rewards.

❓ Question

How can you tell the difference between pressuring your child by offering rewards and celebrating successes?
Your motivation will expose the difference. Are you using the rewards or punishments to apply pressure to ensure the child works hard? If so, you're not celebrating successes! True joy comes from doing something you love and doing it well. That doesn't need an external reward.

Parenting, Interpersonal Relationships, and Happiness

Every day you have the opportunity to model how to have meaningful relationships with others. Are you setting the example of connecting with others in meaningful ways, including your children? Talk about subjects that allow you and your child to connect in a more meaningful way. For example, if your child shares a fear about something, telling a story about a time you were scared can be comforting. (Make sure to include how you got over your fear.) The main point is that you're demonstrating vulnerability and interacting in a mutual way.

Make sure your child has plenty of opportunities to interact with other adults who love him (e.g., grandparent, favorite aunt, etc.). He'll benefit immensely from connections with other adults, people he can rely on both to have fun with and to comfort him when he needs it. And, support his efforts to build relationships with peers. Allowing sleepovers, setting up play dates when children are younger, driving them to a friend's house even when you're busy, and other similar behaviors give him the opportunity to form meaningful friendships. He'll learn about trust, mutuality, and even conflict from such relationships.

Parenting, Optimism, and Happiness

The previous chapter on optimism discussed lots of information about your parenting behaviors and how you can either support the development of optimism or discourage it. The key parenting behavior is how you frame events—are you an optimist, framing events in terms of what could go right and how you can persist to make things better? If so, you're teaching optimism simply by your example.

How Can You Tell If Your Child Is Unhappy?

There are four different things to watch for to determine if your child is unhappy. First, what is his energy level? And, has there been a decline in energy level? Some kids are naturally less energetic—the passive temperament described earlier in this chapter—and thus a lower energy level is their norm. But, if there's been a drop in energy level that cannot be attributed to a health issue, starting a new sport that is tiring, or some other external event, the lethargy may be due to unhappiness. For children with passive temperaments, you may find it easier to judge happiness based on other criteria.

Second, what's her enthusiasm level? Does she show relatively little excitement or enthusiasm about things she used to love? Or, maybe she's never shown much excitement about anything. How excited does she get before going to a birthday party, taking a family vacation, or other similar events? And, has her excitement level waned recently?

Third, look at your child's affect or emotional expression. Does she smile and laugh frequently and easily? Does anything produce real joy or are her emotions a bit more muted? And, have those emotional reactions changed, becoming less common?

 Alert

Monitor the emotional expressions of the important adults in your child's life. Emotions can be contagious—hence the term "emotional contagion"—and research indicates that people adopt the emotions of the leaders. The "leaders" in a child's life are the parents, teachers, and any other adult she interacts with regularly.

Fourth, look more broadly at your child's engagement with life. This sounds a bit amorphous, but the question to ask is simple: Does my child seem to enjoy life? The two ends of the continuum—clear enjoyment of life and its opposite—will be easy to spot. It's the children who are stuck in the middle somewhere that are more difficult to assess. If you're not sure, ask for input from a close friend, family member, or teacher who interacts frequently with your child.

What Should You Do If You Have an Unhappy Child?

First, assess which of the four areas of emotional intelligence that are associated with happiness may be contributing to the unhappiness. Most likely, you'll uncover something related to self-regard, self-actualization, interpersonal relationships, or optimism. Then work diligently to improve those EI skills with your child, referring back to the specific chapter in this book for detailed ideas. Also, talk to your child in gentle ways about what you're observing. Suppose your eight-year-old daughter seems to be unhappy lately. Cite behavioral changes such as not wanting to go to her best friend's house as much or getting nervous before riding the bus. You may uncover some type of situation or event that has created temporary unhappiness or you may discover that her self-regard needs a boost.

A Note about Depression

Sometimes the bout of unhappiness doesn't go away within a reasonable period. Or, the unhappy behaviors become even more pronounced. Here are some guidelines for determining whether you should take your child to a psychologist for an evaluation.

- Noticeable changes in sleeping or eating behaviors, absent a good reason such as a growth spurt
- Lethargy, or low energy that is pervasive and cannot be accounted for by something else such as a physical illness
- Sudden loss of interest in activities your child used to enjoy
- Muted affect, little smiling, and/or expressions of sadness
- Statements of unhappiness, sadness, worthlessness, or helplessness
- Sudden drop in school performance
- Withdrawal from relationships

Teenagers who are depressed also may give away things that are meaningful to them. Teens also can go from very happy to very sad quite quickly, usually due to a break-up in a romantic relationship, bullying, or perceived betrayal by a best friend. There's also a greater risk with teens of committing suicide because they have more skill in collecting whatever materials they need and because they experience disruptions in relationships so intensely they think all is hopeless.

It's always better to err on the side of getting a child help than it is to err on the side of waiting to see if the child will improve on his own. If you take a child to a professional who determines your child is not depressed, that's good news. And you can probably pick up some tips for how to improve his happiness level. And, if you take a child to a professional and find out he's clinically depressed, it's important that you've identified the problem early and are getting him appropriate help.

CHAPTER 19

Mindfulness and Emotional Intelligence

Although mindfulness is not a specific skill area within emotional intelligence, developing mindfulness may potentially help children to improve several areas of their emotional intelligence including their emotional self-awareness, stress tolerance, and impulse control. And, because mindfulness at its core involves being more aware, it shares a key element with emotional intelligence: self-awareness. Keep in mind that the intent of this chapter is to provide you with broad overview of mindfulness and to summarize how it may be yet another technique you could use to help your child build emotional intelligence skills.

What Is Mindfulness?

Mindfulness involves focusing your thoughts on yourself or the environment in the present moment. An important component of mindfulness involves not judging yourself or whatever thoughts come to you. In fact, the idea is to stay so focused on whatever you are experiencing in the present, so that you block out worries about the future or memories of the past. Practiced effectively, mindfulness allows someone to relax by staying in the present moment both mentally and physically. Mindfulness can include being mindful of an object or your environment, awareness of self in the environment, awareness of body sensations, awareness of emotions, and finally, awareness of thoughts, with the more challenging forms of mindfulness listed last.

Why Discuss Mindfulness with Emotional Intelligence?

The goal of emotional intelligence, simply put, is to help individuals become more aware of their emotions and why they experience them, and then to harness those emotions effectively to manage themselves, their reactions, and their relationships. Mindfulness—practiced effectively—helps an individual become more aware and, typically, to relax. If practiced effectively, mindfulness should help children build emotional intelligence skills, particularly emotional self-awareness and stress management.

Children today are experiencing increasing stress whether it's competition to be the best, parental divorce, economic hardship, or parents who are distracted because of work or illness of one of their parents. Childhood stress has increased dramatically in the last fifty years as competitive sports opportunities for kids begin at age four. And, there are literally hundreds of activities that children can participate in and many parents find themselves racing from activity to activity with children who may or may not be that excited about the activity. The hectic nature of the schedule creates stress in both children and adults because it involves another "demand on the body" as discussed in the stress chapter. Mindfulness can help slow things down and restore calmness.

❓ Question

How can I tell if my child is participating in too many activities?
Your child may complain of being tired, ask to have more free time, or balk when it's time to go to one of the activities. A good rule of thumb is one sport and one civic or community activity at a time.

How Is Mindfulness Different from Meditation and Relaxation Training?

There are many different forms of meditation and mindfulness is one form. One of the more common approaches in meditation, and the one most people think of when they hear the word meditation, involves sitting quietly, and chanting a mantra or repeating a meaningful phrase either out loud or to yourself. The goal of such is to lose yourself in the moment, creating a "blank slate" in your brain. Mindfulness, in contrast, encourages active awareness of the environment, bodily sensations, feelings, or thoughts. The goal of mindfulness is a present focus, letting go of the past and future to attend only to the present. Mindfulness can be practiced while walking, sitting, or lying down.

Relaxation training is focused on the single goal of becoming more relaxed and usually involves breathing exercises or muscle relaxation. Mindfulness, although it can result in relaxation, does not have relaxation as a primary goal. Instead the goal is to stay in the present and enhance awareness.

What Are the Benefits of Mindfulness?

Most of the research studying the benefits of mindfulness has occurred with adults. Clinicians have developed programs incorporating mindfulness techniques as a way to reduce stress and cope with chronic pain. And, mindfulness techniques have been used to treat psychological disorders such as anxiety, depression, borderline personality disorder, eating disorders, and addictions. UCLA professors Flaxman and Flook summarized some of the literature related to benefits in adults including:

- Those who practiced mindfulness regularly experienced increases in areas of the brain associated with attention and sensory processing.

- Advanced users experienced a more heightened level of empathy (an emotional intelligence characteristic) than novice users when asked to focus on compassion during meditation.
- There was increased activation in the brain area associated with positive affect (happiness) for novices.
- The stress hormone levels of cortisol decreased faster following a stressful task for undergraduates who had five days of mindfulness practice.
- Couples who had practiced mindfulness experienced more closeness, satisfaction, and acceptance of one another.
- Parents who had children with developmental disabilities and practiced mindfulness experienced increases in parenting satisfaction and social interaction with their children as well as decreases in stress. And, the children's behavior improved, marked by less aggression and noncompliant behavior.
- Relapses for those suffering from depression are less likely when mindfulness training is offered.
- Medical practitioners have increased their empathy, reduced the frequency of taking on the negative emotions of others, and reduced their own stress by using mindfulness practices.

Research with Children

Although research studying the impact on mindfulness in children is still fairly undeveloped, some of the first studies indicate that children may benefit in a number of ways, including a reduction in anxiety and depression, increases in effective sleep, better concentration and focus, less aggression, and better coping with chronic medical conditions. Schools that have introduced mindfulness programs have reported less playground fights and improved control over impulses. Flaxman and Flook also summarized existing studies with children and reported the following:

- Teachers reported declines in anxiety symptoms and academic improvements for children with anxiety issues who had been practicing mindfulness.
- Children with conduct disorder—which is characterized by elevated levels of noncompliance and anger—experienced a decline in aggressive behaviors.
- Teenagers with Attention Deficit and Hyperactivity Disorder (ADHD) experienced fewer symptoms when participating in mindfulness training.
- Middle school students who participated in a five-week, mixed-method program involving mindfulness and tai chi reported they were calmer and had improved sleep patterns.
- Children as young as preschoolers have benefited from mindfulness training. An eight-week training program directed at preschoolers and elementary children found that the less well-regulated children had improved the most—compared with nonparticipants and already well-regulated children—in their ability to self-regulate their emotions and behavioral responses.

Essential

On an emotional intelligence assessment, effectively practiced mindfulness may show up as higher levels of emotional self-awareness, more effective emotional expression, better stress tolerance, or more impulse control.

What Are Ways to Build Mindfulness?

Mindfulness involves the skills of observing, describing, and participating. It can be focused on an object, the environment, a bodily sensation, feelings, or thoughts, with the difficulty increasing as the child moves to more of an internal focus on thoughts. A key aspect of mindfulness is to participate nonjudgmentally. With those parameters in mind, start with an object or something in the environment for the child to focus on (moon, tree, flower, etc.).

Observing an Object

Think about your child and what might suit her personality best. More passive children may want to practice mindfulness while sitting still. Place an object in front of the child and have her observe it and describe it out loud (for younger children) or write about it in a journal (for older children). A more active child may prefer a mindfulness walk around a garden or looking at a growing flower, a car, or your house from multiple points of view.

🅰 Alert

It will be difficult to teach your child effective mindfulness practices unless you actively practice mindfulness yourself. You may also choose to look for local practitioners who offer sessions for children.

Observing the Environment

Again, pick an activity that will appeal to your child's interests or temperament. A child fascinated by stars could observe through a telescope or by sitting outside with a parent. You could take your child for a walk through a garden or during a visit to the zoo, stop at the monkey cage and observe their behavior for five to ten minutes. Again the goals are to clear the mind of what's next or what happened yesterday and observe and describe in the moment. Children should practice being nonjudgmental so that when they turn their attention to themselves they will have mastered how to *describe without evaluation*. In other words, instead of saying the monkeys are "nice," get the child to describe the behaviors she sees. Maybe she noticed a monkey was grooming another monkey or that one of the monkeys approached the edge of the enclosed area and faced toward you.

Observing Body Functions

This type of mindfulness practice involves a child paying attention to his body, typically focusing either on muscle movements or sensations. It can be done in any position, including while walking around. It's more effective to focus on a particular body part or one sensation, such as the sensation in the feet when walking or the sense of smell when walking through a garden. The goal is to be completely focused in the present and observe her sensations, and then describe them nonjudgmentally.

Children who have been practicing mindfulness may be able to focus effectively on the sensation of breathing which may take practice to master. If your child is breathing properly, it's the stomach area of his body that will rise and fall as the lungs take in and expel air. Tenseness can cause your chest muscles to take over breathing. Sit in a relaxed place with your child and be quiet, each of you focused on long, slow breaths that make the stomach area rise and fall. What does your child notice? If you start breathing correctly, you may notice the tips of your fingers getting warmer and warmer. Enhanced breathing opens up the blood vessels more, resulting in more blood getting to our extremities.

Focus on Thoughts and Feelings

Tuning into your own thoughts and feelings is the most difficult type of mindfulness to master. But, it will help children to become aware of their "self-talk." Do negative or positive thoughts and feelings run through their mind more frequently? Do negative thoughts come first, followed by a negative emotion? Or, does awareness of a negative emotion (e.g., anxiety) come first, followed by self-talk that could be critical (e.g., if I'm nervous I won't do well)?

There are many parallels between mindfulness focused on thoughts and feelings and the A-E method covered in the stress tolerance chapter. First, they both require your child to be aware of her self-talk or what she says to herself. Second, they both help someone understand how negative thoughts might produce negative feelings. Finally, mindfulness focused on thoughts and feelings combined with practicing the A-E method to challenge irrational beliefs should enhance your child's ability to increase effective self-talk, resulting in less stress and higher self-regard.

APPENDIX A

References

Bar-On, R. (1988). *The development of a concept of psychological well-being.* (Unpublished doctoral dissertation). Rhodes University, South Africa.

Bar-On, R. (2004). The Bar-On Emotional Quotient Inventory (EQ-i): Rationale, description and summary of psychometric properties. In Glenn Geher (Ed.), *Measuring emotional intelligence: Common ground and controversy* (pp. 111–142). Hauppauge, NY: Nova Science Publishers.

Ellis, A. (2004). Expanding the ABCs of rational emotive therapy. In A. Freeman, M.J. Mahoney, P. Devito, & D. Martin (Eds.), *Cognition and Psychotherapy* (2nd ed., pp. 185–196). New York: Springer.

Erikson, E. (1950). *Childhood and Society.* New York: Norton.

Flaxman, G., and Flook, L. *Brief summary of mindfulness research,* Retrieved September 17, 2012. (*http://marc.ucla.edu/workfiles/pdfs/MARC-mindfulness-research-summary.pdf*)

Gardner, H. (1993). *Multiple Intelligences: The theory in practice.* New York: Basic Books.

Goleman, D. (1995). *Emotional Intelligence: Why it can matter more than IQ.* New York, NY: Bantam.

Kagan, J. (2003). Behavioral inhibition as a temperamental category. In R.J. Davidson, K.R. Scherer & H.H. Goldsmith's (Eds.) *Handbook of affective science.* (pp. 320–331). New York: Oxford University Press.

Kanoy, K.W., Ulka-Steiner, B., Cox, M. & Burchinal, M. (2003). Marital relationship factors and individual psychological characteristics that predict physical punishment of children. *Journal of Family Psychology, 17*(1), 1–9.

Kohaut, K.M. (2010). Emotional intelligence as a predictor of academic achievement in middle school children. *Dissertation Abstracts International: Section B. Sciences and Engineering, 71*(4), 2688.

Maslow, A.H. (1987). *Motivation and personality* (3rd ed.). New York: Harper & Row.

MHS Staff (2011). *Emotional quotient inventory 2.0 (EQ-i 2.0) users' handbook.* Toronto, Ontario: Multi-Health Systems.

Mischel, W., Ebbesen, E., & Zeiss, A. (1972). Cognitive and attentional mechanisms in delay of gratification. *Journal of Personality and Social Psychology, 21*(2), 204–218.

Mischel, W., Ayduk, O., Berman, M., Casey, B., Gotlib, I.H., Jonides, J., Kross, E., Teslovich, T., Wilson, N., Zayas, V., & Shoda, Y. (2011). "Willpower" over the lifespan: decomposing self-regulation. *Social Cognitive and Affective Neuroscience, 6*(2), 252–256.

Piper, W. & Lenski, L. (1930). *The Little Engine That Could.* USA: The Platt and Munk Co., Inc.

Seligman, M. (1990). *Learned optimism: How to change your mind and your life.* New York, NY: Free Press.

Seligman, M.E.P., Maier, S.F. (1967). Failure to escape traumatic shock. *Journal of Experimental Psychology, 74,* 1–9.

Selye, H. (1976). *The stress of life.* New York: McGraw Hill.

Shoda, Y., Mischel, W. & Peake, P. (1990). Predicting adolescent cognitive and self-regulatory competencies from preschool delay of gratification: Identifying diagnostic conditions. *Developmental Psychology, 26*(6), 978–986.

Stanley, T.J. (2001). *The millionaire mind.* Kansas City, KS: Andrews McMeel Publishing.

Stein, S. & Book, H. (2011). *The EQ Edge: Emotional Intelligence and Your Success.* Ontario, Canada: Wiley.

Stein, S., Book, H. & Kanoy, K. (2013) *The Student EQ Edge: Emotional Intelligence and Your Academic and Personal Success.* San Francisco: Jossey Bass.

Websites

Brainy Quote
www.brainyquote.com/quotes/authors/a/aristotle.html

Multi-Health Systems
http://ei.mhs.com

APPENDIX B

Your Child's Emotional Intelligence

This rating scale has not been evaluated for reliability or validity. Rather, it's a way for you to ask yourself some preliminary questions that may guide your thinking about which skill areas of emotional intelligence your child may need to develop. Use it as a tool, *not as a measure* of your child's emotional intelligence. The more often a child demonstrates each behavior, the more well-developed his EI skills are. The questions go in the same order as the chapters, but some of the questions won't be relevant for children age three and below.

MY CHILD . . .

1. Can identify her emotions.
2. Can identify areas where she needs to improve.
3. Likes herself the way she is.
4. Pursues activities with excitement or interest.
5. Tells me what emotion she's feeling.
6. Uses emotion words such as "mad" or "happy."
7. Picks out her own clothes.
8. Is comfortable being separated from you to be with people she knows.
9. Tells me what she likes and dislikes.
10. Stands up to other children in appropriate ways.
11. Makes friends easily.
12. Likes inviting friends over to play.
13. Understands why others may want a toy.
14. Tries to comfort you when you cry.
15. Cooperates with instructions.
16. Follows group rules.
17. Will talk about problems and possible solutions with you.
18. Understands that behaviors produce consequences.
19. Is curious.
20. Resists the urge to overeat.
21. Avoids verbal outbursts directed at others.
22. Can stand in a line or sit quietly without something to play with for an amount of time equal to twice her age.
23. Adapts to changes in household schedules or routines.
24. Moves from one activity to the next without distress.
25. Stays calm when stressed.
26. Reaches out to you or others for help when stressed.
27. Believes "she can" rather than "she can't."
28. Keeps trying even when discouraged.
29. Smiles often.
30. Enjoys life.

Charting Emotions

Directions: It's important to understand your child's emotions, the intensity level at which your child experiences them, and what triggers them. The following chart is designed to help you chart emotions and their intensity. Remember, emotions can be expressed mildly or with great intensity. Sometimes a very easygoing child will express emotions in a mild way and those emotions may be missed by others, including parents. And, while the intense displays of emotion (e.g., rage, terror) are easily noticed, you hope there are only a few things that bother or excite your child this much on a frequent basis. The list below contains the major emotions and different levels of intensity that can be expressed. Observe your child over a one-week period of time and record as many emotions as you can. A few examples are provided to help you get started.

EMOTIONS:

Anger:	Annoyed	Mad	Rage
Anxiety (fear):	Concerned	Worried	Terrified
Embarrassment:	Self-conscious	Embarrassed	Humiliated
Frustration:	Irritated	Frustrated	Apoplectic
Guilt:	Regret	Remorse	Unforgiving (of self)
Happiness:	Pleased	Joyful, Cheerful	Ecstatic, Exuberant
Sadness:	Down	Sad	Devastated, Despondent

SAMPLE:

Date	Emotion/ Intensity	Trigger for the Emotion	Child's Behavior
10.22.2012	Frustrated	Baby sister needed a diaper change before we could leave for soccer game	"Can we please just go?" repeated multiple times
10.22.2012	Ecstatic	Scoring a goal	Huge smile, high fives from teammates, looked at us, jumped up and down
10.22.2012	Down	Team lost	Head down, not talking
10.22.2012	Mad	Not allowed to go home with a friend after the soccer game	Stomped foot, folded arms, pleaded to go

Date	Emotion/Intensity	Trigger for the Emotion	Child's Behavior

Date	Emotion/ Intensity	Trigger for the Emotion	Child's Behavior

Index

We Have
EVERYTHING
on Anything!

With more than 19 million copies sold, the Everything® series has become one of America's favorite resources for solving problems, learning new skills, and organizing lives. Our brand is not only recognizable—it's also welcomed.

The series is a hand-in-hand partner for people who are ready to tackle new subjects—like you!

For more information on the Everything® series, please visit *www.adamsmedia.com*.

The Everything® list spans a wide range of subjects, with more than 500 titles covering 25 different categories:

Business	History	Reference
Careers	Home Improvement	Religion
Children's Storybooks	Everything Kids	Self-Help
Computers	Languages	Sports & Fitness
Cooking	Music	Travel
Crafts and Hobbies	New Age	Wedding
Education/Schools	Parenting	Writing
Games and Puzzles	Personal Finance	
Health	Pets	